I0198185

Uncertain Ships

Phibby Venable

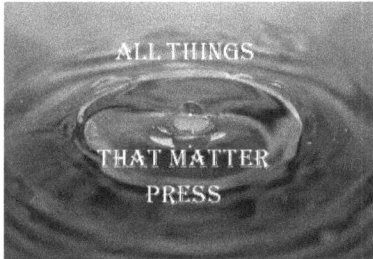

ALL THINGS

THAT MATTER
PRESS

Uncertain Ships

Copyright © 2016 by Phibby Venable

All rights reserved. No part of this book may be reproduced or transmitted in any form or by any means without written permission of the author and publisher.

ISBN 13: 9780996663441

Library of Congress Control Number: 2016933744

Cover Art: June Luvisi (Front) and Marias Arias (Back)

Cover design by All Things That Matter Press

Published in 2016 by All Things That Matter Press

To my mother, who is at this time, a beautiful and uncertain ship.

Acknowledgments

First of all, I would like to express my thanks to painter and writer June Luvisi for her beautiful cover illustration. Her paintings are always exceptional, to my mind, and I am so pleased with her discerning eye to capture the essence of this book perfectly. She is also fun to work with, having a happy disposition, which always comes through in her paintings and writings.

Secondly, I wish to thank Marias Arias for her enchanting back cover illustration. I find her use of color extraordinary and greatly appreciate her work.

I cannot express enough thanks to Marya Berry for her support and diligence, humor, and steadfast belief in my work, which made her collaboration in this book a joyful experience. Her insights regarding poetry, her own primary form of artistic expression, have made her role in this project invaluable.

ILLUSTRATIVE ARTISTS' BRIEF BIOS

Front cover artist June Luvisi

Born in June of 1931 during the hard times of the Great Depression, it wasn't until marrying her college sweetheart and having had four children that June Luvisi thought of herself as a serious artist. She drew and painted from an early age and was awarded a brief scholarship to the Chicago Art Institute, but her parents had wanted to protect her from what they feared would be a life of poverty and deprivation, so they had ruled out art school. She also loved books passionately and earned an M.A. in British Literature from UIC after her children were older and life permitted. Having obtained her degree, she taught English at Harper College in Palatine, Illinois for several years and now publishing on the Internet. She has one book thus far, "Plato and Potato Chips." Earlier in life, after traveling with her late husband to Europe and Asia, she began painting in earnest. Some of the paintings she created at that time, as well as other works, can be found in private homes, schools and churches in Lake Forest, IL. and elsewhere on the planet.

Back Cover Artist Maria Arias

Maria Arias (see back cover illustration) was born and raised in El Paso, TX and lived in LA for four years. She is bilingual in Spanish and English. Since being married and a mother (January 2000), Maria has lived in Champaign, Illinois. Having always expressed herself through color, Maria loves to draw, paint, write stories and poetry, sew, make things with her hands, and, not least, sharing her colorful world with others. As she says: "Seeing others smile makes me happy." It is her aim one day to both write and illustrate her own children's book. She writes and draws for her little girl, and enjoys poetry, fiction, and music. Maria Arias's illustrations have been published in various venues.

"We may have all come on different ships, but we're in the same boat now."

Martin Luther King, Jr.

Preface

By

Marya Berry

"I am large, I contain multitudes" — Walt Whitman, *Leaves of Grass*

"Phibby Venable is a lyric poet to be joyously reckoned with, for her poems wrestle with and reflect, not only her own life, feelings, and vision of the world, but also a vision which is unmistakably American, in its local language, its upbeat rhythms, its irrepressible optimism and, finally, its all-encompassing temperament. Nothing of what she writes could happen outside America, beyond Virginia's Holston River flowing between the Appalachian and Blue Ridge Mountains just outside her windows. And yet, through her unique, inimitable, necessary voice and an alchemy strictly her own, Phibby Venable's poems speak to anyone willing to make life's journey with her, cross the borders between herself and the world at large, that is, speak in a universal voice, to be shared by all."

"Somewhere a mustard sun shines/and azure skies accept the wings/of open sails ..." (From the title poem "Uncertain Ships")

"If that were not abundance enough, the poet, however does not spend the usual long hours of luxurious solitude that so many writers enjoy. Phibby also bestows care—taking upon members of her immediate family, friends and others in need, as well as ensures health and well-being upon 8 dogs, 1 cat and strays of all denominations, be they human, animal, or plant. An exhaustive list of these would underline only too well the poet's commitment, clearly visible in the poems themselves, to loving her fellow human beings and every sentient form of life that she either meets, imagines or creates into being. She greets all of these and this life with magnitude and equanimity. Suffice it to say that on the occasions when it has been my pleasure to talk with Phibby over the phone, a joyful chaos within which she thrives is to be heard in the background. The chaos is not of her creating, the joy, yes."

"I find a harbor that gleams...The tired heart idles in water/and the warmth of salt winds quicken/ in the soft circular air ..." ("Uncertain Ships")

"Phibby Venable's voice is as unique as her DNA. Like every poet worthy of the name, she expresses her unique experience of the world, translating, nay, transforming this experience imaginatively to give the whole (life itself) meaning. It is no coincidence that Phibby writes most often in free verse, for this reflects an inner idea of freedom that she both longs for and creates. Yet there is form to her poems, a cornucopia of vivid imagery using all the senses, natural rhythms (stemming from the nature both within and without), musical cadences, all of which speak (or sing) to a magnanimous idea of personal salvation leading to the salvation of civilization itself. How can this be achieved? Through change and renewal, that is, through imitation of and, even more critically, through communion with the natural world."

I will stand where

all the Uncertain Ships

whisper their longings of destinations

Willing to glide continents

in a restless spray of grace

Rocking my eyes to some new sun

of cradling shores ("Uncertain Ships")

One can readily understand and, more importantly, identify with these lines, for all of us are "Uncertain Ships", find our longings, our dreams, our aspirations at times if not regularly frustrated, mitigated by life's very real limits and, not to put too fine a point on it, limitations. This title poem, Uncertain Ships, sets the tone for the near two hundred poems to follow. There is a general acceptance of hindrances which force the poet (and us) to acknowledge the human condition, with its agenda of tragedy and intermittent joys, and to somehow (miraculously?) transcend it. Earlier in the title poem, the poet describes this experience:

In this ship a prayer stands straight

up against the rails

Fingers loose and leaking complications

into the warm waters of the sea ("Uncertain Ships")

It is only through acceptance of and letting go, conceding to life's vagaries, that one can imaginatively, as it were, pass through them to some other destination, often rewarded by some unforeseen blessing.

"And as to me, I know nothing else but miracles" — Walt Whitman, *Leaves of Grass*

From beginning to end, from the first poem to the last in this generous volume of poems by one of our greatest lyric poets, Phibby Venable stands out, not unlike Walt Whitman, for her recognition of life's prickly (and tragic) side, yet finding grace where one least expects, and therefore worth singing its, life's, praises.

"There is something.../to fool a step into a jump—/A bridge into a trampoline—and who can blame a man/for flying?" ("Berryman Breaking")

Always in this often dark and difficult world in which we all live, there is, along with "...the oil slicks of cars", "the shine of something/too far below to let go of—

... Something as beautiful as the auras of angels/mouthing purple promises in northern lights" ("Berryman Breaking")

This present book of Phibby Venable's poetry, UNCERTAIN SHIPS, suggests a deep, enduring trust in life, as well as a resistance to its blows. Whatever happens—and so much does happen in the brief space of our lives—if we are resistant, courageous, gracious, our efforts to bring light and its attendant warmth into the world will be prized. In the poem "A Mountain Fall", the poet asserts with irresistible conviction:

... I could live with grace—

flowing over my head in sweet rivers

My head bowed with fortitude but sensing

a multitude of bright birds leaving ground

She copes with crooked life by singing its pain, as she would sing its joys. Like Walt Whitman, she does not begrudge life the former or try to sidestep the real issues with which she often finds herself faced.

"I am satisfied ... I see, dance, laugh, sing." — Walt Whitman, *Leaves of Grass*

Finally, I would like to say that these are poems of inexpressible beauty, exhaling greatness at every turn. It seems to me that these are poems of genius, of the American subconscious aired by breathtaking skill, conscious vision and natural inspiration. So, this is somehow all about breathing, taking in and giving back. Phibby Venable's genius burgeons from the fact that she has all it takes to do what she is doing: a gorgeous landscape outside her windows which she graciously makes her own, complete mastery of her language (imagery, metaphor, simile, prosody...), a vocabulary and diction perfectly suited to her themes, innate gifts of lyricism, an inborn belief in what she is doing and, lastly and most importantly, the desire to share with the world the learning process which she would call life, and the beauty that stuns even her darkest moments. In the final poem of the volume, "Night Shades", the poet speaks, as she sometimes does, in the first person about this theme.

I spread like smoke to waver

at the edge of dreams ...

The birds tuck their heads

and songs beneath feathers

Somewhere the night train idles

into a long, last whistle

What remains to be said is that with extraordinary courage and talent, Phibby Venable is able to obey the great Whitman's command:

"Do anything, but let it produce joy." — Walt Whitman, *Leaves of Grass*

Reading Phibby Venable is like eating from the once forbidden tree, now both sanctioned and blessed. She knows both torment and peace and would gladly give of her knowledge. One is never feeling empty after reading her. Her slightest utterance is an enriching experience. I say this from the critical standpoint of her poetry's frequent and close reading. In other words, I could not recommend any living lyric poet more highly.

Marya Berry, BA, MA, PhD studies, English Literature, Medieval Studies

Poet, Author, Editor, Translator, Literary, music, cinema and dance Critic

Winner of the Gulbenkian Literary Scholarship (2 books published)

Former Maître Assistant

Facultés Catholiques de Lyon, Lyon, France

AUTHOR'S NOTE

Uncertain Ships is a book of poetry that leaps from mountain to ocean, and back again. The emotions are as different as each sunrise and sunset demands, according to the day or night, but I wanted to sing a sailor's song of life. It is not always filled with joy, but joy rides the waves in a slippery foothold. And grief will not be outdone, so these poems sigh in the darker waters, but they too have a place in life. Everyone has a certain affinity with ships. Some falter on the ocean and sink, while others sail in a contentment of freedom, still others find the perfect harbor and venture no further. I have traveled by inner tube, canoe, and ship. I know how things fly, and how they sink. I know the sun and the blue-green darkness beneath the water. Still, I hope that if my ship sinks, as ships invariably do—that it will be in shallow water, 100 yards offshore, my eyes finding a tropical island, and a sunlit day of soft flowers and coconuts. And many, many loved ones waving from the shore, where a party is in full swing.

"I'll never know, and neither will you, of the life you don't choose. We'll only know that whatever that sister life was, it was important and beautiful and not ours. It was the ghost ship that didn't carry us. There's nothing to do but salute it from the shore." —Cheryl Strayed

Table of Contents

Uncertain Ships

Somewhere a mustard sun shines

and azure skies accept the wings

of open sails

In this ship a prayer stands straight

up against the rails

Fingers loose and leaking complications

into the warm waters of the sea

I find a harbor that gleams

more brightly than the one before

The tired heart idles in water

and the warmth of salt winds quicken

in the soft circular stir

I will stand where

all the Uncertain Ships

whisper their longings of destinations

Willing to glide continents

in a restless spray of grace

Rocking my eyes to some new sun

of cradling shores

Peaches and Pecans

Looking for peaches on Kings Highway, and slow as syrup
in the sun,

he turned up side roads, private drives leading to luxury,
but no peaches

I wanted pecans anyway—no candied, salted, or colored
ones,

but simple and fresh, a crisp full sided bite of tan and white
flesh

And where to spend the night? Here now on an impulse
drive, and not

enough money for the cool havens lined up whiting out the
heat

I could have slept, the way pups sleep, sprawled on the
back

of anything friendly

He was already undone with sun and some crazy Jack the
Ripper wine,

pure proof that never met a grape or berry—

And I was brooding on signs, so big, so promising with
pecans, mile

after mile of plain handed poster boards—but we never
found the store

And I couldn't drive the straight shift, couldn't reach the
brake,

or jump start a truck so rigged with material things—coke
caps,

a door handle, an odd oil can stationed under the hood

And it was no good to awaken a person in such heat, where
sweat was

a sheet of despair praying for an ocean wind—so I turned
fetal

on the back of the truck—then flipped to my back, knees
up, searching

the sky for every kind of star—a princess with a canopy of
diamonds

A southern sky at night moves perfectly to enlighten

all those soft dreams that go haywire

Berryman Breaking

Some days the black clouds are more than storms

They linger like women in red dresses longing

to be persuaded—shrinking to dark balls that dodge

through the utter gasp of joy to land

in the hollow eyes of depression where sleep twists

to throw an anchor—linger stationary for many hours,

and sway back and forth in a catatonic ad for hell

Depression in the rhythm of blues

An inward wind whistling the hours to lyrics

The sun learning to be cold, too blocked

to enter in the puddles that are made

in the corridors of who cares culled again

and again into horizons that move along the shoreline

There is something white in the eyes

of each of us—blinding sun to fool a step into a jump—

A bridge into a trampoline—and who can blame a man

for flying? I believe it was a sunny day rainbowed

with the oil slicks of cars—the shine of something

too far below to let go of—something to see up close—

Something as beautiful as the auras of angels

mouthing purple promises in northern lights

A Mountain Fall

I am not taken in by your days of brilliance and flowering

dances to the leaf heap

My eyes tire of performances that end

in a quiet smothering of beauty

and the return to a cold earthiness

My face is troubled with indecisive movements

in days that shorten their dawns to dark

I would like some leaping and more sun

A shine so blindingly white that I may look

then look away to form angelic figures

that take their time to fade

I want to look into the sun where circles

turn my eyes into kaleidoscopes

to linger in my dreams through winter

And I want to sing—

Not the songs of the old masters—but new

and purpled with a purity of kind glances

And grace—I could live with grace—

flowing over my head in sweet rivers

My head bowed with fortitude but sensing

a multitude of bright birds leaving ground

Blue Winds

There is a blue ridge wind

with the thrust and hidden leaps of the samurai,

and it is blowing across the top of the valley

I live at the top where all the storms pause

to study lower ground—then fall to touch

on the placid perfection of farm lands

There is something there to stir, to lift higher,

to batter into attention—I am always at attention—

I open my arms to thunder storms, watch the quickness

of lightning and sigh at warnings

Everything here is beautiful—which is a warning

in itself—And the laurels run with the magnolias,

both heavy with scent and mutual admiration

And if the poor here are puzzled

by perfection saddling itself with poverty—

No one mentions it in the storm, and the wind

does not care—And the mountains mist and cry

in the bluish bruise of early morning—

but always fall mute in the majesty of sunrise

Evening Impressions

A last whistle for the dogs

A last whistle from the train

What of a day when the soul scuffs

itself against the body

The grape vines bow in recognition

No one walks this country road

Things cool with anticipation

as the sky gathers its long clouds

into mountains of steel gray

The river offers its deepest water

already warm in the turn of sun

Mist lingering among the trees

A squirrel hesitates to stare

Fox

The fine cut open door begs me come in

To sky and clouds squared off in blue and white

and I walk carefully upon the smooth—

the beautiful—the human warmth of room

And where is she who throws the crusted bread

And calls me pretty girl and little red

How beautiful and cool to have a den

so lovingly arranged for letting in

Hearing Music

The music lives longer than I can imagine

A treble of brown birds in high trees

The air conditioner in a bass of low spirits—

but steady, steady, steady on

I can heal here with the river holding

the stillness of a sudden essence

The ceiling fan dinging the pull chain

against the light—an airy chorus in my head

A melody of dogs munching, pot lids jumping,

a cricket caught in the window frame

and the cracks in this house stretching

to pop time with the framing

The magic of music and the morning singing

liquid slow in the boil and coffee broth

My fingertips rewind the record and words

skate a million moments of my life

across the scream of the ice machine

and in a heartbeat and a breath

a beautiful rhythm awakens to climb

far away from the window of honeysuckle vines

Late March

After your death I kept a picture on the old icebox

that faced the back door and I spoke your name

when I entered the house

I had the spring air on my face, packages to unpack,

a laundry basket of our clothes

Outside the air stayed clean and simple

The long grass cared for nothing but growth

The geese sang over the landscape on the way home

I tried to lean toward astringent thought, live

sparingly, though my imagination was wound

into a long despair, and I had never spared

myself from memories before

But there is something about opening a door

The waiting weight that something more, is present

And I loved the wild geese—flying mate beside mate

toward some long sunlit lake—

Their calls an honest musical of remembrance

Moments

It is dark and all the prettiness sleeps

inside the white owl on a sturdy branch

There is nothing here to do that is

do—able enough to stop the black wind

berating the world outside the window

I have frozen here before winter—

before the palette of leaves color and fall

There are no stars tonight to imagine light

The owl is settled stoic and makes no sound

Outside is a small world fingered by a thumb

Inside my hands shatter useless and can think

of nothing to reach for

This poem is quiet and comfortless

Distant and lost in moments

No Stride is Flawless

No stride is flawless

and mine cracks in the bone twigs

Stone bruises are common

and the wind faces me

The woods are trembling

The wind flings sawdust

in the heat of day

Still walking is an art

I will not abandon easily

I have given all but my eyes

and they have darkened

with worldly prying

and the smooth lies

of tentative survival

No stride is flawless

and my feet are calloused

Still, I am careful of the thorns

that linger in the wild roses

If I could shout something

that the wind could shred

it would be triumphant

as the elephant's roar

and leave the fragile fern shaking

delicate veined sweet faces

Oh Sugar Sugar

So solidly I dovetail into the dark

with my own weight doubling despair

My heart falls down, clangs like an

empty cup and my spirit joins a long

New Orleans parade—

but fortunately it turns suddenly

from the horn blown blues

to a gyrating dance down main street

I leap across the untested surface

of grave stones and gloom

twisting a great vehemence of joy

Singing my triumph, swinging an ax

on the black corded fabric

surrounding me, so that it tears

into the sound of young blue jays

startled from a noon nap

And a white horse, (we all have one)

flies by with a kneel to one knee

and I am off and away

I say, Sugar, oh Sugar, Sugar

and laugh at the flesh

that held such certainty, such might!

Now a cloth grounded with gravity

as I rise in the air of the mystical

into the flight of fight

Small Morning Peace

A morning God sigh in the breeze

Five purple shades build to the top

Fog in between connects the sky

I top a hill to catch a view

Whatever I came here to do

is paused by watching waters move

The sun has lit a sparkler stick

across the calm of Holston's creek

And I am silent as I watch

a small gray bird begin its bath

Intent as any bird would be

before a shake and flight to trees

The Crying Sounds

something so quiet as midnight

folding itself through the window

becomes apparent as the sound

of falling dew that dips a spoon

in diamond glitter, a fragile thing—

the sound of all that craves a glaze

even the moon investigates

its round head plumped out as a plum

the clouds reveal its yellow heart

it hangs in heavy solitude

stars are austere, and unaware

of how the moon grieves loneliness

a flush of careless stars all float

in the moon's face, but they are lost

in sudden streaks of random thought

and lower down I see the line

of mountains full of singing trees—

they sing at night when all is quiet

and as I slacken into sleep

I hear the midnight train—the sound

a hollow warning black with speed

until the dark turns dream like scenes

into a company I crave—and you

with no words carve a sound

that falls between the laughing dark

as I sleep in your stolen heart

The Dance

I don't have to be good at this, I said—

and left the wall—a clinging vine interrupted

from the pressure of a hard back chair

Around the world they were singing

You don't have to cross Jordan alone—I heard

and flew into the music—which could have been

a watermelon—the way it opened into flesh

to fling cool pieces at first and then the

enormous bite of something sweet in my spirit

I wanted to open and spin seeds across the floor

My legs so involved, my hips losing bone

as I felt the haunch of lifting and turning

into something more than upright and moving

Into the enormous sound where I reached

for the horn of some inner perfection

Something ignored rose and shimmied to fold

into some lingering notes

that floated in the air in an aftertaste

of vibrancy and soul

The Fragility of Camouflage

A lizard mingling its whole self

into a shade of self defense

how vulnerable to only hold

off an attack with colored codes

And humans change—sometimes to hide

in order to destroy lives

through war and hunting hold their own

expressing great power and control

But still the lizard—small and swift

seems to have to worst of it

with only his skin to protect

his life from threats and looming death

The Story

I will tell your story as the fireflies illuminate the dark

and the stars grow jealous to watch

It will be in a small town at dusk as the streets roll up

and perhaps a warm rain will beat on the tin topped
building

nearby, though I will add the rain slowly so that the
summer

which had adjusted to drought, will believe the earth is
singing

We will forego the shipwreck of later years, and you will
hear

only the soft whip-poor-will wooing you to sleep, and the
early call

of the deep geared bus at morning—you will excel there

in a comedy of tricks, build your popularity on wit, and
always

sit with the prettiest girls who blush and giggle, and save
seats

where you dally, even then restless, with the yellow ride

You know, don't you, that the stones are coming? That the drugs

will cross your boundaries, follow your years, leap onstage

when you sing, dance, camp on the lonely river that is

never lonely,

the women sliding like peaches down the plate of clay

bank, the dogs

trying to wake you for morning feeds, the wife that martyrs

herself

with leaving, the children who bounce you to laughter on

weekends?

You know it is a landslide, and the alcohol loosens the

mud,

and the losses roll the house into the river that runs to the

sea

And salt—it is in your bones, heavy and melting all the

snowy purity

you meant to hold on to—but it is the high alone, the high

alone,

and the two of us—splendid in lies where you hide with

the alibi

that you can handle it

But you can't. So I will tell your story and make you a grandfather,

kindly, because you are! And generous with affection and tales of

your youth and a stainless steel camper pulled by a Ferrari, Oh,

why not! Why waste a word on your stricken eyes, your stunned mouth,

whispering, If I had known I would have taken better care of myself—

The total silence of a last breath from a spirit that was never boring—

The fireflies will illuminate the dark—I will tell that story.

Sue

I was eight years old, and my best friend was named Sue. We were in the same

class at school and I loved to go home with her. She was the only child of older parents,

who worked all day and went to bed very early. One day she decided to run away, and asked

me to join her. I agreed, so after school we hid in the woods where we could observe

her house from the limb of a large tree. We had a wonderful evening until dusk, when

police cars appeared at her house. Unknown to me, they had also appeared at mine.

The police stayed a long time and searched the house and neighborhood. Finally they reached

the woods where we were hidden, and used a large searchlight to scan the trees.

We were discovered and they took each of us home.

Why did you run away, my mother asked, I was so scared.

I didn't run away, I said, I was keeping Sue company while she ran away.

My mother cautioned me against staying out after dark

alone, and all the dangers. Then

she took me to the drive in restaurant nearby where my

brother worked as a bellhop

after school. He looked nice in his uniform. It was very

white and clean.

We had coke, burgers, and fries—then went home to bed.

The next day on the school bus, Sue showed me her arms

and legs. They were covered in

welts, red and cut open in some places.

They beat me, she said, did your mother beat you?

The thought of my mother giving me anything but a

warning look was foreign to me, but

Sue was so sad, and somehow it felt wrong to say no.

Yes, I said, I was beaten.

Was it with a stick or belt, she asked—

Belt, I said, thinking that a belt sounded worse.

Let me see your cuts, she said.

I lifted my skirt and pointed to a long scrape I had acquired

two days before when I

fell trying to jump from a barrel to a tree limb. The jump

was a success until my hand

gave way and flung me against the tree.

Oh, that looks awful, Sue said, does it hurt?

I nodded and sighed. A sigh that could have been pain!

(Or, the uneasy guilt of lying)

But I never regretted the lie. There was something in Sue's face that needed someone

to understand. The lie was the greatest sympathy I could offer her. And I liked her

sympathy too—an odd bonding that the beatings provided—even if one was a wound by pretense.

This Little Peace

this little peace the morning light brings in

inhabited by golden glints that stain

across the wooden table to a vase

of perfect lilies brought by yesterday

a long bright branch of leaves brush at the screen

strongly swaying in the open breeze

I see the early blue jay on the fence

studying the crumbs flung random in the grass

too little time to pocket in this space

the moments when the sun is beaming grace

the sky blue washed and perfect

in the light

the dream catcher of morning filtering night

Verge

On the verge of alive again

slipping into the unrealized future

I sit up for whiteness, watch it blend

slowly into colors again

Some days I am a circle turning

head over hills to form

a halo of soft colors

There is entirely no defeat

in fortitude, in awakening

into the advanced day

where all the former failures

are still standing

but no longer important enough

to stand in the way

Window

The world is hot with injustice,

and death, and blood

and I did not wish it that way

so he became a buffer and sifted

the things I heard

Until he was dying and I said,

What about trust—(I was afraid,

and no good with discernment)

Trust no—one , he said

(He said it with regret)

but I needed someone—some name

to search for in the darkness

He named a name.

And I grew brave again to think

of one small foundation in the hard

branches that scraped the window

and the new knowledge of standing alone

And he left voices—they scurried

all over the house

I heard them first at the ocean

in the spread of ashes

and when our house flooded and I folded

into the corner of a big chair

Call the insurance company, he said

Grief caught in the wind pried from my fingers

I had to open to a world without lines

drawn for my protection

And you might say I had the trusted name

to chant through the sorrow

And I might mention how I spoke the name

and it proved true

But still in the long run

the numb soul must learn

to stand on its own in the wildflowers and stones

Learning to Sing Hallelujah

each day I stumble more to the south

and to the magnolia, drawn by the scent

of something darkly sweetened and growing

independently on lush trees

it is an individual journey of song

and often the sun sets on my singing

so then I sing bruised blue and gold

and if the sea comes to listen—

if the mountain pauses stony faced—

it is nothing personal to me

it is simply the stoic and steady

leaning into a moment of submission

and something in the spirit

listening for the familiar comfort

of a soft toned hallelujah

Crickets and Trains

The evening is crowded with the aftershocks of the day

All those moments that capsized inside the house,

now slowly pull themselves to order

and grow quiet at the seriousness of dark

With the mountains spilling beyond dusk

it does no good to study the waterfall of words

that splashed wildly through the quarrelsome day

Instead I listen to the late train worry

a long wail through the cross roads

envisioning the heavy fall of warning planks

and the red flash of lights running in circles

It is difficult to slow, to stop for emergencies

although they happen sometimes when the train

is in its breeziest run, unsuspecting, wild

with the challenge of timetables, flying

with the possibilities of unknown faces

Soon the sound hollows back to the frenzied crickets

Their songs blurring in a restless pitch,

tuneless, but intense with passionate complaints

always hidden in the hum of their wings

August Birds

I am not sure of the August birds,

born in the spring and amateurs at winter

The way they wonder what to do next

They reach rock bottom when the leaves

slump and fall into a pile of sleep

They are revealed then and nervous,

spotlighted silhouettes at dawn,

and even they know, there is something

more to them than song, something

they should know and go with

into the endless horizon of the sky

And some do break early for a warmer place

First out of their forsythia nest, first

to break the sky with brave breasts

But I am not sure of the birds by the feeder

Their faith no match for the coming cold

The touch of being parented a deep memory

One that may cripple them if they don't let go.

You With Your Uncommon Eyes

You with your uncommon eyes
Let us walk into this unmanageable day
and brace our bodies against the cold
which is so much easier to comprehend
than the sorrows of ragged sight

Oh, eyes darkened from destiny—
The orbed shadows pause your smile
into a place that morning light finds
and drags without mercy into revelations
you do not wish to see

Look how small the heart stills
when the eyes see little deaths
Stooped bright bird, I will brush your hair
away from your daunted forehead
as the church bells far away
ring a bright covenant against raw thefts

Some Days I Live With A Kung Fu Mockingbird

Some days I live with a Kung Fu mockingbird

that sings a repetition of grasshopper lyrics

and kicks out words, and arms, and legs

I step from a tall cliff and flutter to the ground

and my skirts do not shift for fifty feet

Some days my lips move in words

that will never match or master a connection

and I flit behind and beside my enemies

and shape shift to their irritation

I am a tiger, a crane, a monkey of confusion!

I am a master of the ordinary illusion.

Only, the Kung Fu mockingbird is unbeatable

It uses the modern feat of holograms

and disappears into all parts of the mind

I cannot tell one tumult from the next

No image connects to the one before

and I must search like a miser and sift

through identical grasses—

kicked often by the long legs of disease

bent double with the noise of lost words

'til we are both exhausted and unheard

and I acknowledge my heartbreaking defeat

by the cursed and cruel Kung Fu mockingbird

May 2

It is Spring, and the miniature maple leans its way

through the window—Red leaves flatter the glass

My house is an opening.

The mountain blows up in blue grandeur, and the rocks

are touchable and real

A mystique of birds settle on the piano.

The world comes inside to expand through empty rooms

and of course, there is music—

Sweeping through the back door—fingertipping the wall—

Settling in the shapes of wildflowers

spreading stained glass beauty down the willing hall

I am sitting on a mountain

It should be strong—The edges have held a thousand

standings,

and a thousand falls

I would have you here for the crystal of your heart, for your

eyes that drop to the bottom of wild canyons

and still see light

There is a weariness here that turns the bone to coal

So few know the bird's flight, or listen to a loon

I see few faces, and the day is shy of visitors

At night, I listen to the sound of water many miles away

I think of you in a wine red country—

trimming the balcony with yellow flowers.

Bare Winds

By the dirt road, one patch of flowers,

with soft soil blowing petals down

The wind, no use for a bouquet

blows by as though caught in a rage

I watch them bend rich cotton shifts

Upside down—petals—a dress

And I feel rich to see them dance

Bare winds on fragile open things

With no defense except to sway

And bend with overwhelming wind

I see this often in a world

where all that sways or breaks away

must live with choices that are made

Bare winds most often mean no harm

Exuberant, They simply run

on wind legs caught up in the gift

of all the space that it can blow

But all that sways can later rise

while all that breaks will learn to die

Lighting Candles

Today I miss the candles of a church I never attended

inside a religion I have no claim to—

Somehow, I always believe in the beauty of small flames,

the life of a spirit in a light, significant and amber

An orange tribute escaping the dark—for that one moment

I live at a low voltage—Only my eyes still hold the light

of something unknown, lit young, remaining electric

in the weary strands of ordinary

But there is a music—perhaps the sound is invisible—

Yet, it plays along my journey in a life musical

of highs and lows—a doctrine of light—a piano,

holding a yellow lamp, and softly splitting,

the shadows of darkness

At The Park

Some day virtue may find my legs flying high

in a wooden seated swing—up high, then folding

beneath for the next quick kick out

I will fly too high to be caught

I will not proffer a hand, refuse to offer a seat

to anyone, but the baby nearby—

her leg clutched by the grandmother's hand—

Grandmother whispering, You look good enough to eat!

Baby, so smooth, so soft, so newly consumed by a love

that would devour her, as it protects her

I will throw crumbs to the goose and gander—

who often fight bitterly for small things,

but enjoys them so

And later, if I can find a pure repose

by the vagrant on the bench—I will take it,

having nothing worth stealing, but time

Balancing

If I balanced my soul on my head —

How heavy would it be?

My livelihood, my heart, my basket

of rocks, all lifted in a smile

of abundance

And what if the basket bottomed out,

and I was left standing in the fruits

of my labor — a watermelon bleeding

my family's meal, a pile of rocks

costing my job and survival

The world shrieks with women

wondering, compressed,

high headed with the joy of holding

all it takes to feed their world

Heads extended into vegetables,

fruits, woodchips, rocks

with the fragility of a neck

strong enough to hold bricks

We are all capped with something —

according to our country

If I balanced my soul, how far

would it see—Would it ascend high enough

to see my sisters—Willing and unwilling

lifters of life.

At First The Weather Is Clear

At first the weather is clear,

but the strangeness of dusk is too close—

with moments of sudden gray nostalgia

and the longing for some unknown thing

Then it is dark, and the isolation

of whatever lies behind the velvet outside

grows ashen in the faded sky

Tonight there is no need to watch for the moon

The stars will not open, and the sky shifts

in dark and light shadows of movements

There is that feeling where flight

becomes the adjective of snowbirds

and the songbirds sing them on

You might have been a snowbird

but you sang too long

Beautiful Day

Beautiful day—green struggled back

and lined the trees, protected flowers

bounced boughs in perfect rays of sun

And I was rich—and richer when

I counted children as my friends

And dogs, with eyes alert and turned—

to any mood, or words I spoke

Green and gold, laughter and barks

A swell of richness—each day starts

So much the same—and yet unique—

depending on the wealth I seek

Haiku

the little bluebird

softer than the morning sky

felt suddenly shy

Cavern Grief

there is a small brook

I cull a soft roost in caves

outside the water flows

the wind looks inside

the bats hang high upside down

red eyed with crying

outside starlings sing

a squawk of joyful voices

completely off key

Damascus Storm

Sky crushed in a bruise of deepest blue,

purpled by a storm that boils a broth

on trees so naked boned, so bare of leaves

Valley flooded by a possum rain

deathly quiet, then rushing in to spill

some high strung rage against the stoic hills

Redemptive Gaze

I avert my eyes from needles

There are moments when we must press

our faces into the arms of others—

not look, see nothing but the darkness

which for once, has grown comforting,

and hides us from worse things

Sometimes I must make the best

of the night—be vulnerable in the dark

A dream returns me

to a false landscape of day—

where symbols leap into visions

that fly me, drop me, into a new plane

I avert my eyes in high places—

never look down—look up

where a solid footing still waits

far beyond the hard climbing steps

dropping away behind me

All Winter sickness webbed in black widows around the house

I am tired of the dark trees in naked vulnerability

and yearn for the deep shades of green

I want a soft Spring with sunshine, and evenings of storms

Heavy dark clouds erupting in late downpours on a tin roof

I need the aroma of tilled earth—the view of it turning

in its deep brown scent, the strength and sturdiness of it

All Winter pain rode a crazed gallop, driven by a small, sinewy

man, beating his horses—They stomped hard across my life

At this moment, it is morning—pale pink crosses the dark ridge

The mountain is splotched with snow

The sun is still hidden in her morning rituals—the valley, quiet

February has almost had its day

I am standing on the bandwagon of this opposite hill

waving ribbons and dispensing kisses across the frozen ground

Spring cannot see me yet—she is popping new buds without a sound

A Shriek of Small Crosses

A thousand wooden crosses in the wardrobe,

and the door will not shut

How plain—each dull with a forgotten color

Vibrance rots in the bottom of the stack

And on the wardrobe door, a mirror,

a reflection, a collection of secrets sleeping

in the hard starkness of wood

A someone—a something—has stolen

all the small crosses—and they are shrieking

in the silence of remembrance

They are trying to maintain their decency

past pain and hidden agendas

They are tearing up with the sweat

of abandonment, and the cedar walls

that hold them fast—They mold in the dismissal

of possibilities and turn spiritual

with the penalties of patience

Honey Branch Road

I am driving no place in particular—

Nowhere being a familiar place to us both

We always end up on Honey Branch, with cows

upside down on one side, and boulders leaning

almost into the window on the other

There is a stream, and my mother sings,

Jambalaya, and I'm So Lonesome I Could Cry

The road is a landslide of beauty, the sky

filled with white fog bending into the blue

of mountains, with shapes now softened

The sort of blue where I almost cry, but steer

instead around jutted curves, my mouth a song,

my throat swelling at my mother's gaiety—

She was always this way—the smallest thing,

beautiful, the shortest trip, an adventure

she loved to recall—and I loved to listen,

later, when she was with friends, about all

the fine things she saw—

My eyes are on the road. They do not see her hands,

wrinkled lively tapping time, her scarce hair

gray and covered with a soft white cap—

She has beautiful eyes—like the first Spring

grasses, vibrant as she points here and there

And all the way home, she is singing, or pointing

out interesting places—saying, Wait,

There is another little road we could have taken

Couch View

There is such a terrestrial view from the couch

A comfortable sovereign gazing down the hall,

into the kitchen, out the window, it is an open view.

I am thinking of all the weddings

I have watched from this window

The bridal march blasting through the screen

to the participants below waiting under the trees

Once the needle hung as the bride walked

But later on, none of that mattered, she stopped that day,

but a year later walked far away over the mountains,

some weddings go that way

There was a race party once where we all nearly died

from the fumes of a full blown grill dragged inside

People learn a great deal from near suffocation

And down the hall a thousand footprints

leave imprints of all the scattered hearts

that had the yearn for late and early leaving

This morning I am thinking

of the cradled heads and headaches, the long and short

of backs, braced against the stuffed background

I cannot tell you how much this couch has been around

There are broken hearts, promises, popcorn, and pennies

lost beneath the old cushions, mastering the cracks

Small children have unthreaded the bound fabric

and the tired have slept into the warm wall of it

It is a monument of parties, and slow moments of regret,

but I will say no more of that, sleep being the thing

I need from it now, the familiar sink of rest

Debris

After the storm, the sun kept the smell of dead lobsters,

and the ocean stayed angry, as though shuddering an outrage

Debris lay on the shoreline—and the shoe of someone waved,

stuck up in the sand in a hopeless wait

I went out to write a love letter as the white noise

of waves dulled everything but what I wanted to say

In my head you were screaming—because you always scream,

as though no one can hear soft words

And your eyes always hold nooses that tighten hard as love grows

until the hanging is worthwhile, and a person kicks

the stool away of their own free will

Nothing is calm here this morning—my hair is whipped wild

by the wind and salt lands on my eye lids

Even this love letter has lost its love, and rips away

into the soggy aftermath of a fierce sea

Even When The World Is Erratic

Even when the world is erratic

in a wonderful way

and the wind a cool hand

brushing back my hair

some memory of you harbors

in the compass of my eyes

and I am lost with heaviness

It is only a moment, and never

flinches long, but love,

I enlighten myself with small things

I rub my eyes with the oil

of a stranger's blindness

so that I cannot see

those wretched last days

when all our moments

fell in lost heartbeats

as simple as tattered cloth

unthreading itself

I differ my voice with singing

as bony backed birds

tap time on the ground

With a stranger's eyes

I bridge the wounded gaps

in the road, and plant wildflowers

that serve no purpose

I am not thinking of you now

The stars are spilling

from a black bowl, and a golden circle

surrounds the new moon

Below ground, irises

hump backs of impatience

and thrust upward in the dark

I do not see the lamp

burning its last wick in fire —

a yellow tiger eye flashing

another small goodbye

Hello

I am in the same place

The same objects crowd around me

in the same repetition of devotionals

From this chair I chase

the cadence of bones and birds

and watch so many things turn slim—

Slim being the frail skeleton of a robin

waiting for the worm world

to turn warm

I whistle for the light

of winged butterflies, hopeful yellow

with a streak of soft black

Golden rod delicate on a hard stick

Sun with one bright hand

shoving her arm through the window

Moving To The City

All day moving in and now the street lights

hang like honey beyond our reach

Nothing is settled in, but we can complete

it tomorrow

Meanwhile this porch views a perfect city

entangled in streets that eventually meet

And the hum of a thousand hives

are filled with individual hopes

We come to the city for a new dawn

There is a certain yearn for blue skies,

and the echo of new voices

I sit in a wooden chair and ponder a river

that has never flowed here, never been near

the scream of brakes or the powerful faces

of tall buildings

But I have not left it, and it has not

left me and I am here to consider lights

other than coral and pink dawns —

There is a difference in gray and blue,

subtle and still — a heaviness in the air here

that cannot know the light rising

of rolling fog on a river

But each place we land deserves the view

of a child—a sincere heartbeat of study

When the sun rises high at morning

I will recognize her golden eyes

And perhaps she will visit in her own fashion—

Slipping her familiar fingers

through the porch rails to mine

Musical Fears

I want to be brave

but my mother is boxed in the corner

with a dancing bear, and old music

She is singing my childhood backwards

in a time capsule built for two

I want her to stop

I am the child, she is the mother—

but she refuses all comfortable lyrics

and demands an explanation

for my inability to entertain

It is two in the morning and coaxing

is wearing down my kindness

I shout, Bed time! but she is wise

to my many deceptions

and scorns me with a litany

of how she knows it is day

Even the open door to darkness

makes her roll her eyes and sigh

at my clumsy deceit

Wait till your father comes home

and I tell him you are crazy

It is a warning that doesn't work

in the way she intended

Though it works to remind me

there is no possibility of her comfort

Only the possibility that I will rise

in the same way she always did

in patience and love and lead her

back to the bed

Smiling, always smiling, so that she

is not afraid,

so that she sees the world

is a friendly place,

until finally she is sleeping

and the child leaves her face—

Old, tired, fragile

I am not brave.

One Red Bird Morning

One red bird morning too bright for melancholy

all hard things fell away, and I remembered

the small garden I grew with joy

Perhaps not important to anyone, but if you stare

long enough into the stars, you go blind with belief—

Their battle with the dark becomes

a velvet setting where they live softly in a community

of bright anticipations

And you forget that stars burn, the moon eclipses,

and the way the dark has scorched you more than once

with pain

On a red bird morning it is suddenly possible

to believe in gardens, to see them as a new voice

of courageous birth, a fragile bloom of life rising

out of the hardened ground

I love the soft dirt, the branches and stones, the circle

of life pushing again and again against tremendous odds

And I love the red bird preening in the red sun

One stark messenger of brightness with a wrestler breast

singing from a tree, on ridiculously small legs.

Sensitive

And one boy, holy with hope and imagination—

hunched down in the city grass

with concrete dreams drawn in hop scotch squares—

And his wide song of light grew

into a consciousness of color—brilliant

in the incandescent way of good dreams

But I have entered in the middle of the story

I confess that he is now known as a bad boy—

He robs the world for meth—he whispers

mute apologies—but still he destroys

As another mind folds a beautiful light

into skin sores, bones and blackened teeth

Who gave him ugliness to chew, to sniff, to burn—

What is this broken inside crash

that brings the sensitive to ruin

Suicide

Until the soul—belted—the body leaning forward in a bad
bet—
Terror and tears and beautiful blue eyes, blue skies, blue
stars shooting
in a fury toward bright lights, quiet with immensity
breaking—
And a belted rope with manmade loops with nothing to do
but close down the tent sides of the bright, the long rays
of perfect light—the most marvelous moments of the
magical show
Damn a rope with manmade loops and nothing to do but
choke
the throat to a close and the heart to hope—No hospice for
the soul—
No quilt thick enough to smother guilt, sapling prayers,
the graying shades of hades smoking out laughter
in that beautiful subway through the genius mind—that
could not hide
from vulnerability, rare hungers, an energy unstoppably
too intense,

a nervous laugh, a shattering—a quickening of angelic soul

The Hidden Girl Chant

the words were scared, backed down my throat

and out my fingers 'til they broke

oh floor that holds the words I spill

comfort them back to a skill

at least, the words, at least the hold

of words when nothing else is so

all the beautiful and kind

behind the sofa in decline

I hear the whine of sickly cats

or maybe even worse than that

the giving, giving till I jar

the heavens down and climb inside

and whisper, whisper, little star,

oh little star, oh little star

Nelly

I had a pinto mare, once wild,

broken into submission—she came to us

at a markdown, one blind eye, eerily white

and sporting a bitter disposition

She wasn't like my friend's show horse—

no beautiful markings, no soft glances,

but a style of her own, earned

and remembered in her one good eye

I was a quiet child, partly grown,

longing to step out into the circle,

almost, and yet, I liked the fit of Nelly,

her name too plain, but already familiar

to her, and later to me, and we could be

deep blue together when the sky was right,

or angry in the snow, her fury muffled by flakes

And I kept thinking of her being free—

the way she must have galloped

in the softness of grasses

The way the wind smelled sweet with some seed,

and the sun warm with running

I thought of the man who beat her

into submission, and how resentful I would be—

half of my world blinded, teeth opened by steel

and all the beauty inside hearts and horses

that rough hands can kill

Walking Back

Back by way of a long beach

and the melancholy beauty of white gulls

circling near the foam of sea

No—one walks without a shadow

and I see mine has grown short

as though it means to join

into the flesh and joints

Perhaps it is the noon sun—

tired now of splashing shine

on splashing waves, irritable

at a day half done

Tiny prints lead in and out of the sea

shells broken short of perfection

ride the water as carefree

as all things that do not know

they are broken—I pick them up

when they settle half shell in the sand

I collect such shells on tired days

I carry them long enough

for their hearts to feel chosen—

then leave them to their habitat

of watercolor blues

A piece of plastic shaped angelic,

a sodden cigarette pack, a cellophane cup

A towel named for a motel, a broken crate,

a mangled bird

All trying to be beautiful, to fit in

where they never should

So I search higher up, above the horizon —

where a wild heron lifts off into fancy flight

The beads of moisture on its back —

are diamond droplets catching light

Shortcuts

I can think of no way to follow the mystery

of shortcuts outside the door

The easy aspirations that seem so practical

Short roads, a dozen friendly openings

where I could step in and follow so easily

It is the easy that is troubling

A heart thief leads my spirit down stone

and the large rocks that jut dangerously sharp

I pause to look back and can find no shortcuts

A sensuous wind scented with mistakes

made such a long call on my life

And I love a long road—the carnival that rests

between the weeping willows—set up

beside the river where the stream tumbles loose

The small town streets of elaborate judgments

The freefalls that find no landing

I look for the sacred in the wild

I avoid the shortcuts through compassion and pain

and step instead into a long haul of sunrise

and sunset and the in between of cornfields

city traffic—the abandonment to beaches and light

And none of my angels dress lightly

They are too humane to soar—they trudge

with the jovial and the gentle

At night they paint my feet with milestones

I am a finalist in humor and dance

Eyes closed in a twirl with longshots and chance

The Backward Beat

Your hands softened from smoothing the world—

A white stone of sun lighting your hair

An invisible ruby of wisdom floating

between your eyes

Now there is a cloud charm drifting

across the memories of a century

and your smile quavers from fearful to kind

You mean well—You pleat your nights

with a search for a lost sun

And wonders why the world growls now

at your repetition of words

and annoying requests—

You have done nothing wrong

It is only age reverting its order

Sweeping you backwards toward

a fetal heartbeat—

where your mother smiles in anticipation

and ponders you a name

Outside, the Snow

Snow makes the air visible

There is the clarity of clear

bursting through the flakes

There is the watercolor of gray

in pale blue, as the world here

undresses into purest white

What is more beautiful than the air

wrestling its cool muscle in the wind?

I have a large window where the heat

stares flatly at the flying snow

Warm, but wondering where it is

crisp, windy blasts of flakes blow

I Wave At The Doors Of Heaven

I wave at the doors of Heaven—

Not ready for an inside view,

but tired in the way of things

The universe opens each morning

with paste and pretty scissors

I stick my hopes here and there—

Count ten more often than most

Watch the perfectly round world

tilt its heart into crooked places

At night the universe folds itself

into a dark woolen blanket—

I try hard to sleep in the itch

of it all—

I imagine the feathers of doves—

White and soft with compassion

I wring the neck of hard times,

and hang them to dry with stagnation

But there is no imagination

to halt the traceries of eyes—

Too wide to hope—uneasy bulbs

as heavy as night blooms that close

in the terrible heat of the sun

And the bent backs and necks—

so much more vulnerable than words

What words did Johnny use—

flinging his apple seeds into emptiness

The sweetness always breaking

years after he left them

Never seeing the lushness of a bloom

Merely throwing hard seeds of hope

into a nonchalant wind

Wilting Winter

All winter sickness webbed in black widows around the house

I am tired of the dark trees in naked vulnerability

and yearn for the deep shades of green

I want a soft spring with sunshine, and evenings of storms

Heavy dark clouds erupting in late downpours on a tin roof

I need the aroma of tilled earth—the view of it turning

in its deep brown scent, the strength and sturdiness of it

All winter pain rode a crazed gallop, driven by a small, sinewy

man, beating his horses—They stomped hard across my life

At this moment, it is morning—pale pink crosses the dark ridge

The mountain is splotched with snow

The sun is still hidden in her morning rituals—the valley, quiet

February has almost had its day

I am standing on the bandwagon of this opposite hill

waving ribbons and dispensing kisses across the frozen
ground

spring cannot see me yet—she is popping new buds
without a sound

Rain

The others scoffed, but I had learned

to love the rain—I danced and turned

and down my head, and hair, and arms

rain ran in streams both soft and warm

till I was cleansed inside and out

and all the trees wore diamond drops

for sun is lovely in its ways

but rain has stronger things to say

Walking

I am sewing the silk stitches of air

into a morning walk—

The clouds are out—moving in slow billows

Some are gray with the indecisiveness of rain

The newspaper, thrown in orange plastic,

confirms the threat

If I had wings I could move leisurely,

for there are hills here to travel,

but the morning breath of tall trees

can be uplifting,

and my feet do well enough in wandering

Today I move slowly—I am a waterbird

with water beads rolling down my lengthy neck

There is the flutter of an asylum of ducks

wild with the beauty and power of large feet

They are dipping their heads in water—

lifting them out and upwards in long swallows

Frogs practice the same song—

someone always off key—so that

they must start over

The birds sing sharply to one another

in a rapid shrapnel of voices—

and I am simply walking—and watching

When My Face Cries To me

When my face cries to me, I look the other way

It is aggrieved, wronged, wringing lashes over

the thickness of sorrow

I say nothing—I will not look for trouble

I will not glance at the redness of sorrow

My true lips will not see the others fold

into the sad softness of regret

I am stoic—I am a long silence

of undigested dreams, and staring calmly

into the mirror at a smooth surface

Inch by inch my mind rebuilds

what my heart scatters broken

I cover the whole of it with sturdy plastic

Winter Blue

I am in the melodious south, and white feathers

float on the grandstand—white shirts really—

but shirts with tempo in a slow dance and the women in

boas—

Their heads rising from feathers—Their faces leaning

into broad shoulders—and holding tight

The men have hands that flutter

up and down the soft dresses

The men measure—the women suggest submission,

and the band plays on—usually stretching a song

at the end with a repeat of the chorus

Once I danced just that way, until the owner shouted

It was time to go home—and my partner was warm and

strong

But outside—the air was cold—I could see the stars

were stark and stiff in an ebony sky

And I went from sleepy seduction to a startled awakening

My door handle freezing, my breath a round fog—

The windshield reluctant—a heater loud and blowing cold

And all the stars white in a sudden shyness—hiding

behind the movement of a sapphire cloud

Yes, Yes

Yes, yes, if I knew you, I would be nice to you

although I splinter easily into parts,

and the friend you have today could so easily

stumble, and fumble the ball tomorrow

Some days I live in the grasses, so fresh, so green—

a definite forecast of spring, and yet, a sprig of me

breaks into wooden bones—I fall

I can't tell you the times my bones have broken

into small breaths, the bird mouth gape of them

the silent opening and closing with a sort of innocence

See how I live? this friendly way? this humor leaping

bright eyed into the irony of illness,

into the saddest days of the world, where I grin,

again and again—I suppose I make a good friend

Sincere enough, for all my sudden silences, and so sorry

for the way water beats at rocks to break them,

or maybe the way rocks lift their smooth heads

in attitude, halting the flow of things

Let us lift our binoculars to the pulse of butterflies

Not worrying one another with anything but watching—

Sitting arm to arm, leaning our heads together to see

the monarchs plotting two to six weeks of spring

Sounding Board

Nothing on my blue willow saucer but a tangerine

I am listening to my neighbor spin a trail

of words that could involve pearls if you imagined

her a better life

If I could build one for every sad tale I hear

no one would be left with salted tears

and I could add seas with deep azure harbors

and waves whitened to a froth in joyful high rising

but she is too overwhelmed with the sun's disappearance

and the unreasonable amount of troubles in one lifetime

She brings my shoulders low and I toy with the tangerine

bursting the pulp with a nail to watch the orange ooze

vibrant and willing to reveal its true colors

Her scarf is a stunning dark yellow with green splashes

as though it is the only thing that managed to survive

the winter of her house and rage—the thin lipped anger

at all the things that have gone wrong

and I cannot make them right—she dares anyone to doubt

the total hopelessness of her terrible position

The Couple

One tree has bent, and wrapped itself

around the tall, straight, standing oak

And Sarah thinks it an embrace

The oak gives strength with stoic grace

But Samuel thinks he needs to cut

The limbs that strangle hold the oak

The small, and needy, has a way

Of stealing strength from bigger things

It is the way they live, one looks

and sees a tree that wants to live

The other looks and see a plight,

a neediness, a parasite

This Is A Prayer

This is a prayer whispered from a straight back chair

near the window, impelled by belief and Summer lilies

It is touched by a view of long standing mountains,

and closer up, the way lilies arrive tilting

their lady bell heads in the wild grasses

Something in the beauty seems merciful, and the sky,

blue and large with listening—The free spirits of deer

clouds jump smoothly across the endlessly long horizon

This is a prayer searching for the Heaven of a child

and for the peace laurels by the moist river bank

Some days I cannot remember the words—There is a low

hum of music that rises from the old lily beds and sings

more than my words, than the honey bees, than the

southern owl

The words are white doves that do not mourn, but rejoice

There are silhouettes of birds that fly in the formation

of pyramids, the vee of all forgotten things broadening

as they cross the greenery to disappearing black points—

The prayer is on their wings, and lifting upwards

high hopes of humanity

Thoughts On An Autumn Morning

I saw the sun chasing the Charles, a river stalked

by bicycles, as it rested between busy cities

I watched the breathless Atlantic crashing an immigrant

heart

into a fickle lay of restless sand

A boardwalk extended its artificial tongue for miles

in a jovial shout and seduction to human expectations

Now, I am in the mood for singing and the wine of fall

flowers

I am aware of the emerald pines sleeping nearby,

and the stunted wave of morning rising in a coral crawl

I am feeling tribal and undone, as a call rings

freely through the flutter of breezes, as a twist of fates

roam my spirit in the first chill of autumn dawn

I am in the mood to love the world as it lumbers and rolls

in its heights and flats, and the dogs shiver and cock their

heads in the primitive listening stance of old wolves

Yesterday I was a child traveler, but now I am a fugitive

running a gauntlet of harder to hold places

I slow to enjoy views in the softer way—people standing

more important than possessions, weak kneed dreams propped

with compassion—the morning glories that waited to bloom in autumn—

lifting their soft, simple, faith in defeating cold

The Body Turned Ogre

The flames, surely white and anonymous,

where I could not see them, only feel

the end weight, the fragments of your time

condensed, so condensed! And in my hands.

It didn't matter, I knew you, the heart that flew

long before the burning

I meant to speak of ogres,

particularly the one under the bridge

taking everyone by surprise at crossing

whipping up a fire to consume things

down beneath the wood and stone

There is the childhood fear of something

grabbing a leg from down below

But really, darling, the spirit often disappears

in open daylight, the sun strong and nonchalant,

the eyes open in another world

Here, I was only able

to slip your fragments into the sea

I saw ashes rise on the tips of foam

a wide wingspan of song,

swan song, eagle song,

flown

Tree Surgeon Tale

An hour or so from the beach

Our plans scorched in hummingbird traffic

moving slow motion in ninety degree heat,

a sudden detour sign redirecting traffic

sweaty clothes barnacled against our bodies

in a long wait at a small town light

I saw a tree surgeon loop his belt

over and over up a tree, scaling jump frog

to the branch that had broken—

Twigs dropping in a waterfall, and limbs

trembling beneath a windless cut

He had a captured audience of cars

and in an inexplicable moment swung

to face the crowd, waving one arm, swinging

sideways to grin, but just then

a strap broke and he flew to the ground

in a quiet fold—till a sudden wind

out of nowhere, exaggerated itself,

lifted him again to a soft spruce

where he recovered in loose green arms,

unharmed and held by the grateful tree

treated once by his skilled hands

to a beautiful cut

Waterfall

The trouble with abandonment is the way

it propels itself forward

First an electric bill

or the appointment with a specialist

you believe could be avoided

The old mother, the children dropped

at the neighbors—

The dogs locked hungry in a large pen

Little abandonments build

until there is nothing left

of yourself, a tyrannical despot

Which is why I am climbing

a long path to the top of this waterfall

It is rugged with only small plants

that uproot easily, so that I grasp

at tiny limbs

but they are too young to hold

the weight of the world

so I claw through earth, and my fingernails

break ragged with gripping

all that resists a hold

At the top of the waterfall is a flat spot

It is to the side and smooth with stone

It allows a view of water crashing—

Raging at the hard drop ahead

then falling with forced trust

into a whirlpool of indecisive turns—

Narrowing into a flow that is suddenly

free of choices

emptying into a dozen rivers

finally calm and free to float

Webbed Hearts

I draw my blinds on spidered cobwebs that persist

in their unnatural way of frolicking in the light

There is nothing here for spiders

If the pure, cold light strikes them, let them build

in the window and door

Let their art shimmer in the dew, far away

from my blinds

I add another layer with drapes

so that the certainty of my isolation

will scorn their busy legs, constant in movement

and the endless weave and breakage of webs

My hands are flat on the pillow beside my head

There is the hum of a heater with a fan

and the monotony of sound is precious to sleep by

Morning is clean and fresh outside the window

Not like this house, this human, this dull ritual

of blocking webbed branches, and hearing

too many beautiful birds break for the south

The Sailing

Your pain grew too intense

Your body flung a woman

onstage in ovaries and bloom

You cycled the seeds of life

You took the men into openings

and wrestled a sweet fight

You sang an instinctual hymn

and tried to protect yourself

but an assassin grew

in the midst of your strength

Its name was doubt

Strong, in a world,

that wanted you weak

High headed in a place

that catered to the meek

And you had no conformity

hidden in your eagle heart

No patience for the binding strings

placed tightly on your voice

They called you volatile and cut

your long dark hair

They pressed your shoulders down

and held you there

But you were ribbed deeply inside

with stainless steel

and though they mangled smaller parts

they could not kill

your forward lunge, your majesty

and zest for life

Your face a salted cut of wind

And not contrite

A Beautiful Try

There are so many ways to fly south—

south being a palm tree, a coconut concoction

of the heart

I want to ride on a music note that brakes

for the melodies of goldfinches,

a baby laughing in Marietta, Georgia,

the long line of cotton fields

smooth with old songs

I want to land on lilies and leap

frog the white quartz through wildflowers

When dusk is a plum sky of lovely shadows

and the indigo butterflies rise

I want to watch the lights of a riverboat,

dip once in the Mississippi, and linger

slowly in the warm breath of dusk

When the music note grows tired

we will land on the wings of a guardian—

One already accustomed to my attempts to fly

One aware of my weakness for a beautiful try

At Five A.M.

A purple sky at five a.m., royal with color,
and my body shaped like a question
still too tired to love anything but the window,
and the view that holds only one star

I awaken and wait for the pale blue of day
to adjust itself to my morals
Rise and Shine! Feed, frolic, put the coffee fragrance
into the kitchen, and do good unto others,
no whining today, the red kettle does enough of that—
the way it pressures itself into a high pitched scream
But not me—I am as solid
as a Swiss watch, a Volvo, a mountain rock

Unless, of course, you remember
the body shaped like a question, the eyes shut hard
against the beautiful view—the way my dogs gather
in stares and shift at my folded silence
just before I rise in an exclamation
of daily points and petting.

Bird Praise

a hymn line of fine songs

on the high electric poles

a skyline blue cold

snowbirds tap their toes

to a fresh celestial beat

the group has grown bold

they are fluting sounds

from their own depth of joy

composed in small souls

Unanswerable Singing

Even with the snow covering my thoughts

I am still singing you an unanswerable song

You may hear the trespass of my voice

lifting out of my body to murmur

a litany of fractured sounds

There are flocks of birds overhead

whistling vocals of this time

and thinking nothing of the time to come

Perhaps I am singing that—an emptiness

A long lyric that flies beyond the fluff

of clouds and all the whiteness

of this winter world—to solo in your sky

Sometimes I fold my voice in musicals

and crescendos and listen to the mourning doves

This morning they are on tip toe

and separated by their singing

One moans a silver gray too low to hear

The other answers in a comforting coo

Soon the wind flaps their voices to mute again

Midnight

My neighbor can't see my eyes closing

and I am too polite to go to bed and

just cover up without another word

I feel obligated to hear of every man

who ever loved her—And how she lost

them all—It was her choice, she says,

she does better on her own

And there is a stalker who stalks her

with a relentless energy—He is in love,

He is dangerous—He could be out there

right now, leaning on a tree, smoking

a Pall Mall and breathing deep

Naturally I am exhausted from a four

hour visit, but suddenly—I can see

the stalker in a new light—And he is

all I can think about now that she

has mentioned him—How tired he must be,

and how exhausting the follow someone

who never stops talking—leaves you

leaning in hot or cold, whatever season,

and whenever she pleases

Are you afraid to go home, I ask, trying

to drag up a little sympathy—get past

that meism of the double shift I have

tomorrow—

But, God No! she says, I won't give him

the pleasure of thinking I'm afraid of him

And so we sit—except for the stalker—

who is possibly tired now too, but determined

in his unwanted devotion

Then suddenly, she decides to leave—

Says 'Sorry, but I can't stay up all night

talking

I say, okay, I will let you go—

As though loosening the vise that kept her

sitting in her chair

Stubborn Hope

Even if nothing lived here but ugliness

I would go out each morning and record

my summations

Even if the sun covered herself with

a wool blanket, I would search for pinholes

of light

I would not view the world with detachment

but collect the one blade of grass left

standing, the useless bird nests hanging

from trees, and comfort the wet eyed fog

always uncertain of where to go, what to do

If nothing lived here but ugliness

I would lift a large lamp up toward the trees

to find the lone bird stranded on bare branches

then whisper softly in hypnotic urgings

for the soft small treble it had left to sing

Now She Can Imagine Things Broken

She once wanted a sheltered life,

a blue air, yellow crystals of sunlight

Now she can imagine things broken—

and sees them everywhere

The solid branch of an iced oak

The leaning small stem of a flower

The patient silhouettes of the old

with faces shadowed by sad promises

Humanity sits as an enigma of light

unspoken prayers spilling

from all the wounded places

She once wanted a safe passage,

a valley of flowers, a calm sea—

but some things are meant to know passion—

Raw and rare, raging at the pretty air

and at the apathy hidden

in turned away faces

The valiant burn of an imperfect love—

The lessons—red and tear stained

on lips smeared with shouts of agitation

The stunned look of a scolded child

Disposable dogs seeking out compassion

The way tears crawl up into vulnerable throats

The uncertain sadness of dark laughter

All the words she wished she had spoken

All the fragile dents in things broken

Late Evening Placard

The sky writes in eggplant prose

as the last of the mangoes spill

from the basket

If you stay alone long enough

the world is a placard

of silent announcements

If you watch carefully all the fruit

grows into a universal view

so that soon the bananas are shining

each morning on the last

of the cucumber hills

I grow restless and pace at will

There is a steady drip of water

in the kitchen sink

and no one hears it but me —

It is as small as sweat, but still

it registers in the quiet

I need a catapult, a word joist

to reinforce my back

It is breaking, bending, breaking

one wooden piece at a time

as I search for replacements

along the slippery timber line

He Drank Too Much, What Of It?

The wind found our calloused heels,

but we were too young and too open to care

for blistered feet that healed

naturally—And we were brown

and bordering the sun of exploration

He had the throat of a swan

born to cradle the liquid fire of

forgetfulness—even young there

existed so many things to forget—

When it wasn't silken, his throat

was a pine cone of roughness

with a laugh that deepened in secrets

He stumbled often, called whoa now

on steep patches, but walked

on anyway

Mostly I was a bird of admiration

hiding my face in the outdoor scent

of his steady heartbeat—

And we were as floundering

as beached fish on some days,

unable to lift

a toast high enough to dawn

the shadows of a wolfish world

I loved his determined uphill stagger

His heart too heavy with hope

Eyes he could never wash clear of pain

And a light behind his back

luminous with lightning strikes

The sun painted him gold

He said, Don't ever be too trusting

of this petty, beautiful world —

You know that, don't you?

Don't you, Girl?

The Music Swells

Each morning I startle awake

thinking what an eye opener

what a fine thing

leaving the softness of darkness

Grateful to be aware

once more of everything that

is suddenly mine

Lights! Action! and the way

the music swells

far past pendulums and time

The low notes of the ceiling fan

The high anticipation of bird song

The instinctive knowledge of a gift

A movie that is still mine

And of course I search for

the tender gentleness

of the violin pending

hoping the background of whispered notes

predict a happy ending

There Is Magic

I know ways to seal myself off the playground

and dive deftly into kinder waters

I know the illuminated mind of a child running

through a fertile imagination

There are friends there—great balls of sun,

and ferocious storms all waiting to do her bidding

A childhood is never unhappy if you aren't there

If your clouds turn sugar in your heart and you whip

out a pearl handled pistol and wham the monsters

but keep the spirit, your spirit, in your holster

There are dialogues beyond harsh shouts of disapproval

There are beautiful dresses that gossamer on the ground

and pick the flowers of starry eyed belief

Say nothing bad about small comforts, especially

if you are small and everyone stands tall and moves

too quickly in too many directions—your hand pulled

along too quickly for a firm step

There are pinpoints of light that is offered regularly

to the innocence of children and the children glow

at the one lie that turns out to be true—

There is magic! There is magic! and it is you.

If You Love Me Sane

If you love me sane—how will you ever find me

when the stubborn hairline recedes and my head opens

to a broken axle

When my simple thoughts turn buoyant and fly beyond

the gateway you have adjusted so carefully

And a madness that is alien to your love comes out

in a small hum rising

Flinging words like shudders, like joy, enormous

with emotion

How will you grasp me when the clasp breaks

and I drape myself in vulnerable despair

across the neat world you continually handle

Will you rearrange me? Straighten my folded covers?

Will you fear the cloudburst inside my rooms

or find a boat and ferry us beneath the broken moon?

The Thing She Was Best At

The thing she was best at was riding

the ticketed train that gloomed its way

nightly through her small town

It was a black train and she complained

that it never reached the sea —

But no train ever did to her knowledge

And definitely not her train

which could not run on the sun and sand

but flew through stone and over dark bridges

She was the sort of person who never

purchased a ticket, but slipped into

the open doors, where things were loaded

that were never meant to be hers

And there was a beauty in the black night

A sheen that hardened on water and softened

in the wind blown shadows of trees

Sometimes she traced the graffiti

of mysterious places — placing fingers

in paint that had dried some place far away

Her eyes a wind burn from leaning out windows

that were always locked heavily

during the day

I Confess No Large Thing

I confess little because my eyes shut

in pools of darkness where I sleep

with head—on dreams

The world folds into something manageable and longings

no longer domestic, but brimming with the song

of chaos and the long leaf pines sweeping

vividly against the window

From my bed I can see car lights, trucks,

identified by the height of their muted glares

so that I fall unconscious with the sight

of hope on dark highways and of journeys

I know the ripeness of winter on cold panes

I turn the electric blanket up as though

I have an answer for everything

But really—it is so small here most days

And I am an avid liar creating

mud pies of prettiness with small fingers

I shape the pies circular and smooth

and ignore the tiny pebbles that persist

always in the ruin of yearned attempts

I dream I am lost in a crowd of people

who brood openly and speak into my face

with words that blur and they will not repeat

anything, simply stare until I awaken

half worried, trying to remember a sentence,

a word, mumbled so softly

by someone, somewhere.

Gray Birds In The Lap Of Winter

The snow birds are feathered gray

by the weather and blending into

a landscape strung along high wires

so that they appear to be standing

invisibly balanced in the sky

as though they stopped

in mid-flight and are now considering

directions and wind shifts

Perhaps there is no wire and winter

holds them in his lap and ponders

the food shortage in their small world

or the miraculous undertaking

of gray birds to survive at all

with their large vulnerabilities

New Day

There is electrical tape for the frayed cord

of the heater, but the ceiling is too high

and the heater too tired to try

for new heights

There is a window with a view

of streets and cracked concrete pretending

to still be a retaining wall

There is Amos sitting in his inflammation

of joints and bones that make themselves known with

painful regularity

And Anita, in the kitchen with floured hands and a slight

limp that has earned

her self-proclaimed contempt

She brings Amos his cup—more cream than coffee, more

hand heat than thirst

and they watch the city morning dim street lights and blare

horn alerts

Arthritis weather, he says, and she nods an agreement—

then suddenly they both

grin—roll their eyes at age, and watch a new day begin

Balancing

If I balanced my soul on my head—

How heavy would it be?

My livelihood, my heart, my basket

of rocks, all lifted in a smile

of abundance

And what if the basket bottomed out,

and I was left standing in the fruits

of my labor—a watermelon bleeding

my family's meal, a pile of rocks

costing my job and survival

The world shrieks with women

wondering, compressed,

high headed with the joy of holding

all it takes to feed their world

Heads extended into vegetables,

fruits, woodchips, rocks

with the fragility of a neck

strong enough to hold bricks

We are all capped with something—

according to our country

If I balanced my soul, how far

would it see—Would it ascend high enough

to see my sisters—Willing and unwilling

lifters of life?

Cross Ties

I secretly seek miracles in the sun and moon—

It is a lost art—open to ridicule

Small morning glories,

and yellowed honeysuckle vines

tangling their fragrance here

in a mystery of strong roots

I can say nothing—simply watch—

Step out the door and know

the praise of bird song

until the first crumbs of dark pretends

to cry its dew

And I see the two

of us—white shadowed as stars—

A smaller space between us

The long ferry of night

waiting to ride us to oblivion

where I capture your attention

in a moonlit river call of love

In the first blanket of the fall

and the drawn out drawl

of the nine o'clock train

wailing to us from a loneliness

of cross ties.

A Cross Of Roads

In Carolina at a dirt cross of roads

I saw the splendor of a star shine and fall –

It was autumn and a ripeness was pungent

in the dying leaves—the moon large enough

to reveal golden petals of indentations

There was a coolness in the air and a thickening

of night sounds—the owl running

a compulsory call—some lone bird

I had not heard before rolling a long

sound of woe

And you, barefoot and suddenly mysterious –

more than my best friend—suddenly a flower

crumbled and thrown down in faded leaves

Our houses faced each other and the roads ran

four ways, as though we had choices,

as though the traps set by the captured wives

of the Methodist church would never reach us, but run

confused

by the choice of directions

There was a beautiful boy who broke beneath

the iron will of his mother, her disappointment

more important than the open light in your face

There was a denial, and a new knowledge dawning

in the insufferable night—and a baby too small

to hold up a fist

And you, beautiful meteor of the bright, dulled

with realization—crumbled with a sharp stick

and the smell of death

No longer worried about the plans we kept

hidden in the red diary beneath the iron bed

White—a broken laurel, an ivory face

searching the stars in an endless stare

Dusk On Holston

Layered pink through ink spill dusk

another day has given up

to starkness in a desperate cold

that chills a place beyond the bone

and I am quiet in private thought

and wearied of my dialogue

with heart and hands and body heat

with work that islands in my blood

the bitten lip of careful love

I need to place my coat aside

and seek instead the warm surreal

to form a figure undefined

to melt the ice caps of the world

Walking With Sandpipers

Harried dodgers of the sea

The brown autumn of sand birds

move back and forth in a frenzy

of findings—their bills sensitive

and probing for survival

Let the baritone of the sea rush

warnings and swallow the world

The sandpipers scatter backward

only to race again and again

into the edge of a sea

that uncovers temptations

in a friendly glee—

with only moments for digging

between crashings

Walking The Morning In

A cherry daiquiri has spilled

across the skyline where the rain

weighs heavy in long bodied clouds

And I am too still in a house

where all the noise has been tamped down

and silence lingers in its lines

In my white shirt, bird seed remains

from feeding brown birds yesterday

I have forgotten how to change

my shirt and other various things

And four o'clock, and soon now, five

pace back and forth and peer outside

Nigh In The Wrong Watercolor

The spotlight is on the old star who disappeared

several years ago—There is a comeback planned,

but in this movie time runs out

I turn off the set because I believed up

to the final scene—and now she is simply gone

Maybe she married a millionaire—old movies

are prone to marrying off the heroine—

after a great deal of tragedy of course

After they realize it is night in the wrong watercolor

And the small stars have grown pointed

And the producer runs off with the money

that would have provided the old star a good life

The paint is red ochre—hell fire red, desert earth

red, until a cobalt blue fills her broken heart,

and all the plastic wrap peels off the picture

But maybe there is a twist—and the paint smears!

Suddenly Stewart and Armstrong

edge out of the matting with a wonderful life

and a wonderful world and see! Someone is dancing,

whirling all the way across canvas to end on one knee

Oh, he is holding out the flowers—He is a tuxedo

sparkler, and look at her—Hair up in a turban—

One hand touching her cheek—And in a moment,

her swing coat swaying straight into a love song.

In this poem, no watercolor goes wrong.

I Was Bleak

My first music was a locomotive

It panted pass my window at five sharp

Bellowing a wail of melancholy,

always out of breath

and hurrying through the dawn

in steel misgivings,

weary with the weight of flatcars

It made me tired.

And the second sound of the sawmill,

frightened, the shrill shriek of a maiden,

the saw biting into board after board,

a penetrating sound that shook the trees,

already nervous with the wind of trains

And I was bleak,

drenched with the fine mist of coal dust

always sifting through the artificial light

of our gray houses

I lived as such moments passed

in an upswing

toward optimism and maturity

into snowstorms where I waved my arms

in the pristine snow and made angels

that left their shadows on the earth

I fell asleep easily with rain.

The Morning Is No Longer What It Was

The morning is no longer what it was

a blush ago when I stepped out the door

It may, however, now hold something more

The sun in steady climbing brings a change

A cardinal flutters at the windowpane

He sees his image and prepares to fight

a phantom bird that mocks him in the light

That is the way I often fight myself

My nature sometimes overcomes my sense

and I am driven to relentlessness

with old mistakes that brink and edge my eyes

so that I cannot see what lies inside

and think instead a rival rules my head

and comfort is a gray quarry of lead

The morning now is more a brilliant shine

of incandescent streaks of the divine

And I, too often shadowed by myself,

ready for the sun strikes and the light

Standing In Salt Water

The sea holds a reputation, choppy,

frothy, unaccountable, and diverse

but I cannot be worried

with the futility of that

A quiet gull fancies my shoulder

A fisherman brings my tray

I have a gift of gauging islands

many miles away

Nothing here is self-important or

distressfully intense

I steer myself past alcoves

bordering regrets

The shells are not unbreakable

running with the sea

Some days the sun falls in the sand

and I rock my song to sleep

I am always watching

the horizon stretch to flat,

the way the water slaps

forward, forward, back

Do you know a secret?

I heard this from a cloud

or perhaps an old man drifting,

that moved light, like a cloud

Learn to lose your feet

simply by standing still

a meditation of shifting

deep inhales, exhale

I Am Passionate At Crossroads

The trees sharpen up the dark ridge

where the black bear lives

nonchalantly, unafraid of anything

And I am envious and sad

at the lack of fear—knowing as I do

the many dangers of confident beliefs

The way elaborate lies spin off

perfectly gorgeous lips—the way

prayers muffle and mumble at times

in the sharp thrust of aggravated living

And I envy the heavy certainty

of the bear in cold weather

needing no supplies but her fur

where she curls her head into

a complete surrender

What harm can come?

Who will bother her there in the depth

of sleep that dreams only of awakenings

How beautiful to dream only of spring

While here I am standing at a crossroads

And all the directions lead to caves

both familiar and strange with decisions

I am passionate for a circular lair

where I might meet myself again and again

Lumbering strong and warm in a true direction

Lifting trout with a triumphant roar

and proclaiming a victory, a fresh water win.

Absorb

Do you think we pass each other

and nothing occurs?

It is impossible to walk through

auras unstained

Even with eyes averted, and thoughts

scattering into shop windows and stores

The soul grows big eyed and troubled

It absorbs the colors of auras

Small silverish lines hold us upright

A royal purple softens our standing

Inside, as we pass by one another,

there is an understanding that kernels

into the deepest background of the eyes

And sometimes we pause in our inner landing

with small lights blinking stars of unity

that will not glisten or die

Sometimes we smile.

Vacation Vacancies

Beautiful steps down to the sea

until I am in a sun splash of shifting water

barely holding my balance in this vacation

No sunlight can touch you—a hard flint

silhouettes your face—and the water

is a long turquoise tragedy of your past

I am the wrong woman, walking

into the December of your air space

For she was here many times—standing

right beside you—her eyes filled

with expressions, and saying things

you could not hear for watching

the peach movement of her lips

Eventually you condense everyone into her

Paper dolls, wavery women, each bearing

some piece, or flow, that you believe

belongs in another sky, golden, fleeting,

You curse the stupendous mistake again, and

again, but it never ends, this curse—

this loneliness—an endless beggar wearing

your heart to rags—raging at imposters,

and something lost each morning

as you sober to realizations

Beach Song

I already knew Sunday morning would be larger

at the beach than in the steady valley

The valley in early light is silent and deep with greenery

The trees too slow to unblacken and bloom

Here is a different pilgrimage with a view

Already there is movement—the shrimp boats trailed

by the steady hunger of gulls—the endless dives

of big beaked birds, and the water pretending

it has been awake all night, and perhaps it has—

flinging its frothy self at the sand that pretends

a demure indifference, a tease of sorts that rushes

out at the sea, only to return to sunshine

The red lipped stain of a Styrofoam cup has caught

the attention of scavengers who believe it may be

something

worth eating—a rare seafood that manifested in the night

There are the fortune hunters strapped with detectors—

they appear to be searching for water, but seek gold,

and the careless blanket's absorption of jewels

falling into the master cover up of sand

I see the real gold is up over the horizon, a red lava

ball bouncing above the fingers of the sea

Once I took a photo of my daughter from the pier

as she stood in silhouette facing the sea—she became

an ebony figure facing blue, a dark image whose body flew

forward while the shadow girl stayed

Some days I am a shadow too. I am not fearful or at peace

I am more the conch shell ignoring fast water and stoic

with sun

One small cut and I become a blowing shell—

trumpeting a bittersweet solo from a mermaid lost at sea

Ex-Wives

Insert thirty years and we are friends

by familiarity

Your life hinged with mine through marriage

Finally seeing each other through the vacancies

left by one we both loved better

but could not keep—A fated hand waving

that quick smile and famous goodbye

An awkward personal knowledge of the same man

and a drawing closer as all leave who know

the memoirs we are speaking from

Now you, now me, and a cold winter's walk

unfolding in a summer essay we read

to one another—and smile—tentatively

Jealousy buried in a suit coat

Something softer in your smile than I ever saw there

Perhaps we will be happy with this make do—

There had to be a reason for him to love you

If I Speak Too Often Of Morning

If I speak too often of morning

it is because the sunrise

blushes her face with rose

and lifts upward in a gray

that sprawls in several shades

across the mountains

that are waiting in bruises

of lavender and blue

And I am stunned by the roll

of stone hills far away

and an army of wild trees

that always seem

to be headed their way

And the fine mist, the fog —

the eternal morning wash

of it all

As though the sky wants me to recall

day after day —

Some remembered scene in words

Some simple morning prayer

Complicating Things

If I dive beneath

still waters

If I am quiet

and watchful

a healing will come

as I stand dripping

in the warm creek

waiting for restoration

The doe on the bank

is casual with interest

She is chewing grass

and enjoying the sun

She has no plan

for a fine healing

Grazes instead

on a fine day

Outskirts Of Longing

What are you talking about, he said,

Sleep is as easy as anything gets.

There is a breeze outside, and the entire

window is brimming blue and light through

the house

I have a written complaint with fatigue, and watch

shows behind my eyes he cannot know

because I am a swamp flower and he is a man

used to stretching out anywhere with a

flirt of knowledge in doing what he pleases

But I have to till sleep, scratch it across the face

quieten melodies and soothe the gossamer

that moves too quickly to ever allow

the feeling of permanence in my posture

And there are alligators swimming

in a decorum of vicious tail turns

that love me as imperfectly as all do here

I am trying to be friendly, only because

it is easier to bring peace back, only as a lure

to polite separation from reality

And I pity the spirit captured in my body

hired as a sentinel, always on guard, threatened

by my heart's hitman who lost sense some time back

and now waves a gun at any marginal movement

What are you talking about?

I love you, I reply, my exhaustion dressed as a draft dodger

waving small hands in its explanation and yearning

toward peace

And I smell absence all over this room, and a woeful lack

of sincerity, or even worse, an ineffectual dove

dead still and white outside the window

feather by feather dropping in pauses

And a swamp with dull green currents

rolling slowly across the half trees hanging

out of the ugly water to remind me once more of sleep

So I tell him something beautiful in a last breath

in a sluggish softened voice that dissolves truth

If you will be quiet for a moment and watch the wings rise

The river loon will fly.

Tattletale

He summons help from social services,

but his mother smooths the questioning brows

with sweetness, and she is simply trying

to raise her child—He is dulled

by watching her eyes and her arid breath

covering him with the spittle of deceit

The officer leaves and her fists are ready

flailing, breathing in and out with rage

at the sight of him—ungrateful, small,

but powerful with telling tales—

He will not tell again—She drinks with

her friends—crying over and over

how he lies at the least thing—how she

tries to give him everything—

And the sympathy goes on—while he is stashed

conveniently in the upstairs closet—

His eyes never growing accustomed to the dark,

but seeing so many things—the way everyone

believes in a smile—and in a lie—

They will not uncover until he dies

I keep spelling my name the same

I have dangled my head and my heart,

widened, lengthened myself with change

All my attitudes have altered

in the night and I have awakened

new and improved with hindsight snug

as a newly washed wool sweater

But I confess it does no good

And the cold brings tears of joy

or confession, or solitude

where I meant to make friends but felt

compelled instead to make

life easier for a few dogs and one

cold eyed cat that I knew well enough

to know purred frightened behind the farce

And the farce was a pale knitted gray but the cat

held to it fiercely anyway

I scraped criticism off the bottom of my shoe

Stood with my hands by my side

as vulnerable to the wind as a cotton towel

whipped wildly around an outdoor clothes line

Some things have a way of wrapping

Some things warp or tear over time

It's true—I have reinvented everything

and pieced myself anew

Especially into the sting of morning where I gasp

at the fresh orange bursting in the sky

and the juice flying loosely into the green trees

and the sometimes terrible beauty when young birds sing

and I lean into the song and blend

a waiting crowd into myself

I have been caught in a vase of crushed wings.

I have been stroked and toughened to change things

Mountain Morning

Dingy linen wraps the mountain dull

Even the dogs are listless on the rugs

Almond twigs stick silent from a branch

as though touching a sun is in their power

but stiffen, and stay frozen in the air

That is the general mood that holds the day

but still, I think a walk is no small thing

and want to see the way the houses smoke

in chimneys that reveal how others dwell

in fog that drifts and looks across the hills

Then clears itself to vapor as fog will.

Desperation

Don't let me die, she pleads

And I say, I won't, I won't

Her eyes big in a bony face

My eyes dark with the horror

of deception

I would write a eulogy backwards

which is the way she lives her life

now that the mind refuses to stop

all those tiny sparks

burning, leaving

I would push all the wreckage

to some finer place and work

with my most concentrated diligence

but I cannot

do anything

So I comfort, kiss, hug the broken

into a recognizable whole

even if I have to live in the past

even if I am no longer a daughter

but everyone she ever loved

sitting here in her stories

and answering whatever they might have

answered and proclaiming the power

of life and death

tight lipped at the sly

tauntings of life

My friend paints herself into a corner

She knows the real tsunami

is the blinding fog rolling over the ridge

It moves her way in a destruction of fragility

She has a pristine showing of muted blues

and a still life graceful with silence

This day is no mongrel

This morning she saw masterpieces arranged

with an eastern slant of light

She watched the purest paints

standing perfectly still to become champions

She painted the blue ribbon crawl

of the suffocating fog

into one tightly contained corner

In The Crazy House Of My Heart

In the crazy house of my heart, a line formed,

a thousand lies lounged in the sun—a table nearby

held tequila and the colors of ocean fresh umbrellas

A crew of working men packed ribbons of pavement,

but I could not see where the work ended

There lay the broken loves, bandaged, smelly as

old fish, but cheery, and recovering nicely

A childhood ribbon, a black snake I once jumped

over on a sudden path—the coarse mane of a palomino

rising into the air, again and again, on two hind legs

A fudge ripple cone by the railroad tracks—a train

forming a cross, moving in four far flung directions

There flew my spirit, pedaling an old blue bike with

a basket, and a spill of marbles and magazines

Oh, crazy heart, kaleidoscope kinky, and still kicking up

fine soft dirt roads—so lively, so stoic, so impossibly

breaded with roses and wild vines

Oh, dreams crushed to sand, and laughing waves

pounding

the foolishness of lost footholds—Oh, Hurrah! hurrah

again! And all the bleached bloodlines redirected through red passion, and family, and friends.

Beneath Smooth Waters, The Swan Is Working

In sunlight, there is nothing but perfect flow

Black eyes languid, white petaled fluff unruffled—

but the spirit knows

Today I meant to ponder—water off a duck's back—

but the swan is so graceful—it reveals an almost limpid

disinterest, while the feet quivers a fury of hard won

balance

Yes, I see your presumptions—your belief that I flow

But always, there is rough water, a hidden element

in the nerves—topped by the sun's gold

Bells In The Valley

I am halfway home, but the bells are ringing

in the valley church, so I wait for the sound

to echo through the pines—

The notes drift through, as though God is blue,

and I am rich with a longing that refuses

to be named, but settles in deep places

This is a narrow road, but beautiful in the dusk

The young squirrels are quiet, and the soft sound

of water dropping from rocks is musical

This is the time of evening when stars line up

in vague outlines of golden promises

The timberlines begin to slip into mountains

of their own, and the horses that have not gone home

shape into folded silhouettes of prayer

Perhaps they too are listening to the bells—

Ringing their confidence until even the smallest,

wildest of hearts, have hopes that swell

a longing of faith from their valleys

An Ending

It is a cold night in Carolina, and the room is dark

Our window is worried by a broken shutter

swinging on one side in a hapless flap against the house

It is not the only wound here—the bureau drawer vacated

before we arrived, and the shower is a shy spray

that on some days decides not to show

There is an abandoned game of solitaire, and a crumpled

can holding up the window while you smoke

I can see the swinging light of a bulb on a wire, and

the neighbors bush hogging a dead tree—the noise we

welcome in the silence of this room

It is too cold outside—too cold inside, the blanket thinned,

the wall heater a halfhearted red and black—

And I can see stars, connected to nothing, yet hanging

with perfect poise—as, occasionally, a black cloud drifts

by—Perhaps it is our true testimony riding languid sho

gun in the night sky

Roy Saying Goodbye

A delicate gray wraps the hills in ribbons
as birds call out from hidden places
You spur the doctor's death notice, but not
the fact of it riding so hard in your lungs,
and refuse the penitent face, forego grief,
and come now to tell everyone good bye
No—one mentions death, and all pretend
a good humor, so that you must think everyone
polite, but foolish somehow, missing the point—
Playing at pretense—while you can pretend nothing
It is March—time for the South to turn again
toward green grasses, and the warm winds
that tan and tease toward ocean beds—and here,
are the honeysuckle preparing themselves
for hummingbirds, and the sweet scent of life
Everyone tries to say something with a gathering
of outdoor chairs and a bonfire in the back yard
They slap your back as you flinch, and warm your hands
in the golden denial of family and friends
But what is there to say? To know?

You are sailing away to a foreign land, and everyone

fears the name of it—Everyone avoids the permanency,

the lack of existing as who they are, who you are to them

They love in the light of dawn, but the dark is so far away,

and no one wants to say something that might be wrong

You talk it their way, and take the love they are desperate

to deposit, but fumble frugally with uncertain hands

And your eyes, so sad and golden brown,

match the smile on your lips as you grin all around

telling jokes, and drinking toasts with the liquor

your cousins brought from town

Light Through The Window On Plums

This is where the star dust falls

in particles of window light

The plums burn crimson, then relent

into the red of peppermint

And everything I have still white

dances in that striking light

Light through the window on the plums

it stirs something I can't discern

So soft, and pretty on the plate

I love the colors that they make

Why do I search for something more

Than plums, and stardust, dancing sun

Whitman Transcending

What if we are all large, and filled with multitudes

Today my daughter claimed, her angry self,

confronted a cruel stranger, and that it was her one

of many selves, standing up for herself

Inside each spirit is an individual who steps out, defends,

gentles, grows full soul to challenge the world

In this way we are never alone

Whitman spoke for the multitudes — their faces

of slavery, rights, religion, love

all slipped through his pen into words that filled

an avalanche of vacancies

How could he help but see himself passing —

lungs shriveling to a painful close — so that he shouted

with poems — swinging his large head, always worried

by the beehive of voices

And when he flew, he claimed, nothing would be left

between his hat and his boots

You Believe In Me

You believe in me—above the noise and chaos,

bridges that swing and break with the weight of our words

Everything grows spiny and fragile with breakage

Still, you play harmonica with a country grin,

Your hands black with swiping at all the repairs

And the guitar has a loose string—the music out of reach

in the wide expanse of this house

The money that goes away, the hand carried letters

I lay like court evidence at your feet—

I have the names of the dead growing on my back

All the praise songs are out of breath

And still you point at the open sky, wide eyed, believing,

I have the fey luck of the Irish, a nice laugh,

a disposition ready to please—As I cup my hand

around a child's crayon, marking x after x on the

calendar—

Biting my lip, and nodding, pressing so hard the color

breaks in my hand

Is It The Longest Day Of The Year

It is the longest day of the year

and I can find nothing to cling to

but a hand mirror, and a dog who runs

back and forth in the sand—

Tongue lolled, ears back, eyes excited

with the possibilities of water

The hand mirror is something

I found in the sand—marbled, broken,

a lie of blue reflecting the sky

Everything here disguises itself

with sunlight

It pretends that beauty is enough

And the waves are magnificent

if I disregard the bodies

preserved in salt by the sea

And the seashells pretend to be unbroken

until I pick them up and stare down

at the pieces left in the sand

And the sun rises in a red orb of promises

on frivolous beach balls and abandoned towels

as the gulls gut one another for pieces

of a sandwich left in thin grass

If I lift my face to the sky

I can taste the sweat of old brass

in the hard pressure of a breeze

and moisture, and damaging heat

I watch it slap closed umbrellas

that cannot break free

White Gold

In Saltville—named for the salt mines—

Skeletons tell of the last ice age

and of the Chisca of the sixteenth century,

who are now long extinct

Battles were waged for the salt works,

vital to preserving

meat for the men—but then,

history here is sprinkled with salt—

And the ground gives way in places—

once taking down highways

for the taste of smooth blue

in its mouthy embrace—

I worked in the town—

but grew afraid of sudden openings

The white scratches of death swallowing

my car whole—I feared the fake domestic

in the hard crust of the mountain—

And Appalachia whispering, Salt of the earth—

salt in the wounds, salty biblical warnings,

Hardened cream and white linen

The earth yawning for the taste of highways

And the wind—A mimic of the ocean,

but moving in the dark, slipping out the mine door,

into the essence of a wild, high, green leaved sea

And the low crumbling sound

of mountains perched prettily on hollow ground

December Sunrise

Honey rolling upward and over the hills

Rich and unbearably beautiful

in the white sheen of snow

The fluttering moths are gone from the door

All summer they clung in a longing

for the enticement of yellow lights

The trees are nude with veins varicosed

through long stark limbs

Eventually everything reveals itself –

And I can see a long way off

Now that the trees have emptied themselves

Now that the view has widened

to the steady rise of morning sun

See how the snow is sympathetic to solitude

and spills a hopeful purity against the raw

Lending its mystical cloak to the stark

Whispering—Soft, soft, soft.

Mercy

There is a night train with beggars

hidden in an empty car

Their voices are singing in the common

key of C

There are cobwebs in the car

and a thousand stars staring in

through the small windows

They can see that the universe

is full bodied and black

and how the trees wave

in long lonely bends

They are hoping for a quiet exit

when the journey ends

But for now a song trembles

in a joyful movement

It is not uncommon to be happy

at finding an unknown destination

warm in the exhale of companions

When they stop there will be a landscape

of common C's

humming all along the streets

to the stranded

Things Glimpsed At Eleven O'Clock

Things glimpsed in the dark at eleven o'clock

flicker behind outlines and window frames

There is the incipient monster under the bed,

and the feet secured—the arms wondering,

what next, and the new reality of silence –

It was never this loud before

But once confronted—once the shadows

fade to vague—there is a new view

Now there is a transient in the room

It is the new you brooding on a dark steeple –

No, a garden hat, propped on the wardrobe

The ability to constantly recreate ourselves –

give names to the nameless—believe

the right attitude will tame the dark to darling,

lingers, and there are patches, which are windows,

that show it is brighter outside than in

And that is what the fear really is—that star

you failed to swallow—the warm glow

that never sparked—the beggar heart that worries

the inventiveness of thoughts—and that beautiful dream

once hatched on the playground – wandering

somewhere nearby, but never found

Feeding Sparrows

Clannish in the chilled morning

sparrows wait for the week old bread

with quick eyes and narrow heads hidden

in small coats of down

They place the dice of their lives in winter

on those who feed, fling seeds and things

into their frosty paths

They are clinging by a song, and winging

in the hardened morning snow

with a lack of fat for warmth

and small scratches at a ground that gives

up nothing I can see in the transparent light

And I am nervous of small, dependent hearts

standing with certainty in the cold

folding like small prayers on ugly limbs

with such a simple faith that all

will go well—And if it doesn't

I never want to know

if a bird of such simplicity dies in the thick snow

I don't want to decipher how songs fly

across the lone star morning to starve

still singing in their small coats

I don't want to see songs stutter

in such a trusting throat

or freeze in the pale light

of what they may have believed

was such a pretty day

Walking With Maria

I could have told you that the fragile cannot stay here

but I have a voice of connotations and broken hope

that murmurs low with nuances and scattered words

I cannot say a thing as perfectly as I wish it to be

It's not for me to tumult the sweetness of a dream

I have grown shallow on the long road, hope only to bring

small equalizers here in slippery words

Walking slightly ahead of you, I try to space

obstacles as far from you as I can in this place

Letting Things Go

If you come to me one day with your journey voice asking

if I remember anything—Did I take it seriously?

I will nudge the purple lily in my heart now white in

places—

cough softly on the small dirt roads caught in my throat

and remember you always in the jaundice of the moon

I am a slouch in letting go—and clutch the deity of truth

with small hands—Each year smaller still—but never

imperial

to those who fashion long careful lies—Then ask that they

be true

If you come in your free spirit too lonely to thrive—

Empty now and listening for something real to own

I will take you seriously and nod at your apologetic tone

Quietly agree that you had no choice

Even your gauzy eyes that hate the things you do—

I will take them seriously too.

To A Northern Poet

You with your anchorman's voice

so enthralling to the southern ear

As though you have the world

lined up in order and the next

series of world news will be delivered

in precise and comfortable detail

I love when you disc jockey low

and the words roll

in the perfection of an English

I cannot know here

where slurred implications

are followed by suggestive looks

that could mean anything

In the south we have a problem

with clarifying things

Friendly Goddess

There is kohl out lining her lids

so that people might find the way to her eyes

where a yellow fades palely beneath

of past problems, a jaundice of men brooding,

a third eye now watching the world with knowing,

without wincing—And her eyes smile

a dark caramel of crosses—an immortal hope,

and a hint of underlying humor

They tell her there is nothing funny

about her situation—her medium's view

But she is not laughing at that

It is the entirety of the journey—the apprehensions

that humor have killed

It is the way chaos falls over and over again

but only hurts once before she laughs

The Seasoning Of Self

Age alters things and I become accepting, gentled

The way the pelican bears the brunt of a bad nose

Too heavy with weight to drift air

but settling into the softness of smooth wings

My body is patient with me — a lover overlooking

imperfections — Perhaps seeing what was once there

My face is not stone — it loves the road

It spends long moments drawing tiny maps to show

on bright summer days

But I am almost threatening with happiness

My mind flutters open and shut with the seasons

A tiredness takes hold of my body,

but cannot seem to capture my mind

I am suddenly more aware of the vulnerable and kind

The Stories

I am giving you back your stories

now that you are too sick to remember

the way you told them

I find them in this broken place

Put the pieces in order

And you choose one

We watch the camillian memories

and admire how their colors change

smiling when they match your eyes

If You Love Me Sane

If you love me sane—how will you ever find me

when the stubborn hairline recedes and my head opens

to a broken axle

When my simple thoughts turn buoyant and fly beyond

the gateway you have adjusted so carefully

And a madness that is alien to your love comes out

in a small hum rising

Flinging words like shudders, like joy, enormous

with emotion

How will you grasp me when the clasp breaks

and I drape myself in vulnerable despair

across the neat world you continually handle

Will you rearrange me? Straighten my folded covers?

Will you fear the cloudburst inside my rooms

or find a boat and ferry us beneath the broken moon?

This Book

no matter how often I open this book

inch line after line with my finger

the story remains a blur of voices

a quick change phantom leaping

just ahead of my grasp

over and over I am interrupted

with mundane cries of negativity

always at the part where

the character pops a light bulb

in a life ah-hah realization

of some new and perfect plan

Whistling Toward God

Whistling toward God in a snow white body

In a rush of red and yellow and black and white

A large brown flurry of dusty feet

And all is forgiven of the betrayal of self

I leap upon a star and whistle so hard

that the pearled gates shake

and the sleeping stars quake

And I see the hand of God pressed

against the all-knowing lips

and recognize the high pitch

of the whistle I could never do

Not alone — Not by myself

Even when I ground my teeth together

and whistled short hisses that went nowhere

He was there — He was there

to answer sharp and clear in the brilliant blue air

February

In the restless chafe of February

a residue of winter lingers

There is a dull final wait

as the sealed flowers awaken

to a vision all their own

Inside boisterous spirits

a longing pastures for spring

Once more I shift

the weight of seasons, and cull

an order from the past cold

Some are missing in the pale gray

Irreplaceable hearts have slipped

into the void of lost voices

No nuance, no syllables

can imitate the ones gone

Outside the robin circles

and vulture wings fold

Sudden Days

Suddenly I found myself with no place to go—

Of course I say suddenly because some vagrant

dancing blood, some restless impatient red

flows through my veins—But it was not sudden.

Not at all. It was a daily glance around

at the gaining of shadows in the hostess heart

of the house—And the shine of mahogany dimmed

with dust—Soon it was simply myself and my mother

who made good company most days—especially

the ones where she was polite to the stranger

who never knew she had out worn her welcome

And of course the dogs who would stay

with anyone purchasing a meat, or possessing

the ability to pull a kill from a box

beyond their dexterity to open

But now, Not too suddenly I was alone

watching the comedy channel as my mother

flirted outrageously with the comedians

making gestures her way, winking, exaggerating

their eyes in the sudden clinch of a punch line

No place to go, but a nice moon floating like a charm

A bright new penny, only pleasantly yellow,

lingering outside the window, larger than stars

a lightbulb with big ideas and good intentions

In the mirror before bed I saw small ruins

softening into my face—which may have been

love lines, but possibly a trick of hard lighting.

Will There Be Something To Keep Us Warm?

What if we get there, and the birds

have flown to another point south,

and the weather has turned cold

Will we wrap in a blanket

on a balcony facing the sea

Will we watch the heavy lines of rain

fill all the man made pools

as a gray storm screams an outrage

through the ragged long haired palms

Will we be blown beyond the language

of the too high waves translating

torrid sounds of uncontrolled thunder

in the crazed lightning as it dances

across huge mounds of crashing sea?

Balcony

I stand on the balcony believing I can lose

myself in sun—In the guilty pleasure of being

alone with myself, unreachable

for just a moment and unshadowed

in full view of a wide open sky

The world is an avalanche

and buries me in snapshots that grow

older by the day—I am tired of it

and blowsy with hot sea wind turning

my hair to a hornet nest wrapping,

flapping around my face which is upright

for a moment, impassionate and still

to the impossible promise of freedom

There is a seagull rehearsal in front of me

Wild dives at anything edible and a white

winged viciousness that hunger brings

I have something to say to myself

but cannot bear the strain of listening

when the water is crashing so beautifully

I impersonate a figurehead of old wood

A goddess head plowing the burn

of confrontation with speed and sea

The plane high above me streaming

a colorful tail of oysters on the half shell

and something else in the small print

that I am too sky blind to see

Stumbling Toward Grace

If all is one, I may find some grace in that
I look hard enough for everything to show itself
and correct my puzzled misconceptions
A homeless friend said he was happy with stars
and a lack of taxes—and eligible for social
security just by existing
Yesterday I found a small dog exhausted
with searching
for the car that dropped her and sped away
She wasn't fast enough to catch them
Like a love that hopes it is all a mistake
holding on to a certainty that
they should have moved faster
I have a fence that would have fallen long ago
except for the morning glories
twisting and wrapping
And I have grace—some place—
hidden in the temple my eyes built
of crumbling brick and shiny plaster

A Psalm of Moss

As I walk I see a psalm of moss caught

in between buildings

It has managed to break cement, and open

itself to this place that rests

in shade most of the day,

as though it believes

that somewhere in this bare hardness

someone might need to stay on softness

The sun strikes here rarely and floats

white peacock feathers against the walls

but it seems enough for the moss

Perhaps it is too imaginative to say

that moss believes in anything—an organism

lying still in an alley—And it may be

that it is only me believing in things

I often wish for soft stops on hard rocks

longing for both the stoic and strong,

and a soft comfort for thinking

There is a man nearby on the street

offering to lighten my burden of change

Hopeful that I will not remain weighed down

with something that may loosen

the stitches of my coat

He wears a thin jacket with his fists

in pockets holding it together

against the cold, and clenched

against something only he knows

I do not know his story

but there is a coffee shop nearby

and the wind is slapping us both to tears

Some days I wish we were all

simply human and handing our change

to one another—Singing a moss psalm

through every high wind

A large cup of coffee warming our hands

The Viewing

Finally he is still enough for them to stare

at the last image of a man, and study his rough hands

waxed smooth white with a shine

Now that he is stretched with artificial stuffing,

and embalmed bloodless, they come to see

what he is made of, more approachable with

the keen, dark eyes shut or missing

But quiet is all Nancy Jane can think about

She is clutching a ragged doll on the front steps

and listening for his deep laugh

She lets people pass by and enter the house

She pulls on the plait of her too neat hair

Only six, but even she knows, he is not there

Listen

I know you are in one Heaven or another —

but, Listen, you were right about planting

the wild honeysuckle too near the rose

The honeysuckle won, and the rose is gone

And also about weeding out the young trees

that flew in on wind voyages as seeds

I liked their free spirits, but now

They have shaded out all the light

and darkened the house.

Lay Me Down To Sleep

The news channel blasting, with lines going across the
bottom
like a child trying to say everything at once
As my angel, exhausted in its search for optimism
props its chin on one wide wing
I am trying to wean myself from the past
and grow accustomed to all the new things I need now
The night places the moon on a pedestal
and I watch the bright circle for inspiration
The angel is watching too, both of us weary of the news
and neither of us bold enough at the moment
to acknowledge the other
I am probably a disappointment—There are stars out
tonight
loaded with entertainment and fireworks
that at the moment appeal to my fancy of Heaven
But the angel probably knows a thousand places to go
far beyond my humdrum imagination
And it is Sunday—Maybe we should do something
magical,

spiritual, inspirational, but instead I stay inside

and nothing good is playing on the movie channel

and the angel is serious about its position

and guarding me through the fears of night

Of course I love that! But I am restless, and the moon

is the closest thing we have to ponder

I am getting sleepy and feel the slide of darkness

closing out the long day

Falling finally onto the down chest and the short breath of

sleep

as the angel's head droops, and the night falls deep

Considering The Horses

Strung out in the lonely stanza of a dusk song

I am considering the loneliness of horses

As though I am certain of the fact

At night their legs appear too delicate

folded between the heavy bodies

What does it take to be a horse

running suddenly into boundaries

Surely there are some that jump defiantly

over fences that do not hold them in

as much as the stable, the belonging

What if they sicken suddenly of moderation

and leap into what might be

an opportunity to fend for themselves

What if there is a hobo wind

brisk and clear with blue air

and a thousand grasses scenting their choices

beyond companions to an impulse

they suddenly have no desire to halt

and to the wind, sweeter than a hay stack

whistling promises through the night air

Cassie

No one is home to answer the phone

There is an unknown gallery in her eyes

Her lips restless as a river

A pretense sings in the voice of her lover

I cannot explain her to you

She is temporarily some place else

She steps through a wide expanse

of all the broken things so closely strewn

She is raw in the woods without a talisman

and totally small by the overgrown birch

Talking With The Baby

It is a small thread at first, snipped at birth,

but you land on your stomach, and your knees

You pull yourself upright and try not to lose

all the balance that is inside you

There are stumbles, falls, an uplift into arms,

a bitten lipped learning of boundaries

And there is love, a blue ribbon trimmed in gold

and brass bands, and brass rings

And sometimes, people, too hard to hold

The Quietest Prayer

The quietest prayer I spoke

was just loud enough

to echo back a negative answer

I did not say a word

or protest the imposition

of a solid no

The sun warm on my face

My hands squeezing questions

I had to carry home

The Storm

It was a sunny day of pansies, and

the sun had grown absent-minded

by the heat

until it was all a dull arid wave

of hot shimmers

I was low slung and fatigued

with the hammock thoughts of shade

so when the storm came

I simply watched the black rolls

of clouds racing, and the thunder

belted out like a sergeant awakening

the troops—And the lightning raced

in a frenzy of sudden disturbance

I could see it behind

first one cloud and then another

I was in the worst place I could

possibly be—under a tree

I had the uneasy sensation

of something missing—a dampening

of hopes lost to humidity

And the lightning, and the thunder

grew more crazed and cross

And the storm grew more and more

angry at itself

But I was too tired to hurry in the house

The pansies were dropping and petaling

down, and the hammock was wet

and close to the ground

Until I was a storm in a body of cloud

eating the lightning

and slurring my words

in a wind that heard nothing

Not evil. Not good.

Emptying Into The Sea

I urge the long rivers to empty my spirit

into the waiting sea

I have an alliance with the rivers

Each year I hitchhike into the peace

of beach side accommodations

and pledge my fidelity to the wild

waving from green fingers and blue

The sea knows me from other days

I sleep at the edge of its world

and waves race close enough to cover

my feet in frothy welcome

There is nothing in particular

that others might see

But I am broken shell and perfect pinkness

I am rock, gull, sandals, odd debris

The tiny coral flowers

dancing an entanglement

of rich emerald arms

The broken seaweed scattered

by an undaunted storm

Incandescent Sun

A bird is dreaming

on a stem of yellowbell

above dandelions

Small iris mountains

push the grasses of cover

to a purple scent

Spring no longer hides

her delicate intention

of awakening

The sky forgets gray

in a blue and white movement

Incandescent sun

I Harbor An Idiot

I harbor an idiot inside my head

so you might as well come in

Take a seat on the teeth

ground flat and comfortable

or fun slide down the long tube

that swallows everything with a grin

then dances to the tune of raw reflux

Or climb a little into my eyes

sitting in a smudge of white

watching the world with an amazement

that is not so much mystical as hopeful

Longing for a hard core but sheltering

a thousand vulnerabilities

and one idiot still believing

in the intense stare of a child

waiting for the story to end

with a high flying hero

My Mind Is Drinking Heavily

My mind is drinking heavily of the champagne dusk
A pale apology ending a day where ice and snow
fell brilliantly for long moments before melting away
and the sun flew out as though irritated at the display
Even the weather has lost its moorings

But I say nothing, simply watch with empathy
and pace back and forth beneath the black limbs
Somewhere inside I believe a healing lies in disarray
My heart snapping open in the pop top of a can—
Perhaps sardines, the way things stack in neat rows

I should arrange my emotions much the same
but I am fighting the feeling of watching myself
An anonymous mind curious at the woman
under the limbs—The woman captured in the house—
The grand promises of an autobiography I can never
convince to work itself out

There is my bewildered mother at the window

She waves and mouths come in, come in

Both of us runners with a well-loved understanding

Listening to a concert of disgruntled voices

Singing a baptism uncertain as blue jays

Waiting out the gray rains of wind

Wolf Winds

The air so soft and lavender

with wolf winds slipping through the trees

My aspects dance on stiffened limbs

Yesterday, at Pearl Head Creek,

a water laced with pure white stones,

I saw a mountain woman's face

She hunkered where the water ran

to gather in a gallon jug

enough of it to carry home

Her skin was lined, and Irish fair—

threads of red and white streaked hair

The eyes she lifted to my face

where calm, and clear, and full of light

But somewhere in the depths I saw

the blue of bruising often found

in those who have surrendered ground

She had the look I've often glimpsed

of grief grown calm and motionless

Yet still, the wide, evocative smile

of one who thinks of much to give

She did not say an unkind thing

simply remarked upon the stream

and how the water ran so clean

And running clean is what I thought

I think it often when I see

Tired hearts that walk with poverty

Crushed beauty in their once young lips

A different crushing in the eyes—

where long lost hopes have stepped aside

And still they smile, and still they smile

Walking The River

You believe I will speak of blue, but no,

a pale green, an emerald, a birthstone

that believes in fertility

all float in a canoe of good intentions

When I look behind me, there are past passions,

a gathering of decades, the fragile bones of a fish

tagging after another year—

And always, there is the river,

curving around the bend in a question,

washing the long hair of the weeping willow,

the stoic legs of a loon,

seeking the lazy owl, who closes

his eyes on purpose

If you look closely there is a map around my eyes,

a small drink of water in the palm of my hand,

and a coastline I built, from small cocoons—

the ones that never opened, never flew

Early Touch

a solid morning

opens its fresh step of dance

on the moistured earth

somewhere a city

with unyielding ambitions

somewhere a temple

rings its bell of communion

here a soft blue hope

lands on black lashes of night

to flutter a dream

You Were Hearing Voices

All those moments of staring that your mother called
epileptic
One corner of your mind a madhouse, in the other you
housed a multitude of voices—they read you unsigned
letters—played themselves off as familiar, as you twisted
for a name
I brood upon you, and see a darling, never subtle—blurting
a desperation and always, an uncanny wisdom
All the ruin that leaned into your best laid plans—
The silence filled with foam, and you listening, listening
with your beautiful eyes! Mourning doves lived there—
They fluttered in your lashes, and cried in low moans
And in your heart—the breakage
Cold hands, your mother said, warm heart—
But you always looked past her, and bore the chill
Once too often in the midst of beautiful outings, you left us
with parted lips—eyes fastened on some other place
They found you later in the creek bed
Looking upward—watching water through empty bird
eyes

White Sunrise

This morning there is a white sun rising

on the foggy borders of the hills

The sweet breath of delicate honeysuckle

and the weightless warning chill

move adrift in the lessening leaves

This morning there is a long blue ridge

a copperhead of rolling length

and more fog than I've ever known

and a white sun tiredly shining on

I think of how I meant to take

this summer into beach front shores

and linger there, my head flung back

to converse alone with the salted air

This year no beach was near enough

to offer rest or breezed caress

This year time raced into the world

and spun the season on toward gold

before I had a chance to sing

a summer song in bands of foam

What Were We

What were we with such fervency?

The Arizona trip, you know, with tumbleweeds—

How they would blow—us more than free

And Highway One, we meant to go

from Florida on into Maine—We planned

to keep the sea in sight—

We had such ephemeral times—

Yet stayed together all of lives

Or all of yours—How could I know—

That no one else would want to go

I met another man—he flew,

a private course, and thought us old,

too old to leave our safety net

You would have laughed to know of it—

To see my face, startled surprise—

the stunned amazement in my eyes!

But no, I think your words would lean

more toward my side in sympathy

I saw a fog this afternoon

that settled like a cloud gone blue—I watched some geese

point toward the lake—I found a pointed arrow head

I stood nude on the balcony, with only a blanket

covering me—I danced about with music notes—

I showed no one the poem I wrote

Then I grew listless and I stood—

and watched the neighbors burning wood

Soon in the dark the valley glowed

with fervency that turned to smoke

Wet Woods

I am beneath a tree in the wet woods

where rain beats down a crush on everything

that might grow wild, or try to rise above

some thought of what the storm considers good

One moment and I ply my hands with thought

of saving one small patch of violets caught

outside the meager shelter of a tree

I reach to touch, but then withdraw my hand

No ministry of touch or reaching bough

can save so small a thing, I give it up—

Too many things need saving, but the rain

is beating in a gale of angry swings

And I have grown indulgent now of death

what I can't change I hope now to forget

But suddenly a flutter I know well,

a stubborn disregard of all that fails

rages in my body and I curl

all that I am around the beaten flower

And what of gales, and hails, of all hard things

After the storm this one small patch still blooms.

The Dog Sees My Sleep

The dogs see my sleep as a betrayal

They shiver with huge cotton mouths

and nudge me with reproach

A cold sword nose pushes for someone

to be in charge, but the mistress sleeps

past a thousand miles of servitude

I am awake in another land, and riding

the open air of a horse lope

I am in palm fronds and edged water

I feed nothing but this affliction

of desertion that shatters light

and runs a wakeful dream of beauty

Not unsmiling, but merry past the point

of all old music, I will keep coffee eyes

that question nothing, and a mount

that leaps through time

I will return in the morning with clean skies

to feed the hungry, and the sick, and dance

to the motions of a clannish world

Then the dogs will be sleeping, unaware,

as the soft twin moon doubles behind itself,

two headed and quietly crowning

Slender Psalms

There is the white noise of a fan

ruffling the summer curtains to a dance

of endless night

Outside, the rain is a culvert of rushing,

and I am going nowhere but here

Once on the street, I saw a child hand

too little money to the ice cream man—

He said it wasn't enough

and I thought of things that crumble, a smile

being the worse—the anticipation of joy

mocked into submission—the mouth

suddenly uncertain of its purpose

White noise is also that way—it brings a lull

so that the brain believes

it is resting—that the world is a hum,

a straight line refuge of monotony

Awake, it is startled by slamming doors,

the overflow of technology, and long moments

where silence turns into the sound of crickets

What is lonelier than the things we lose—

The blackberry patch of dreams too black

for the picking

Faces skimming in and out of our lives—

The small sleeping hands of children

The flinching eyes of abuse

And of course, it is true—that we grow

weary with the dusk of trying,

and the ruts of rain flowing into long nights

But still we hold high

Such a yearning of song

Waving toward hope—

Such a slender psalm

Rue

the shrub that bears small yellow flowers

that makes one nauseous with its power

when dried it brings a cure to cramps

causes abortion on request

both good and bad, like all of life,

double edged as butcher knives

Pall Bearer

Intermittent scent

of snow in the cold, sharp breeze,

and your arrival pending on weather

and whether you can still make

the existing flight

They ask you warmly

for a certified time frame

as if it is snow

that stands in your way

and not the hard black

time to say good bye

again carrying

an offering to the ground

of someone whose heart

painted your past with sunlight

now a solid weight

you will lift with stoic love

Winter hearted mound

another absence to bear

in the holy singing

Paces

It took so many days—I turned

to a preservative for ruin

I kept my patients warm and dry

tranquilly I touched and salved

But I love fields—I know that this

is really of no consequence

But there they stretched so plain and wide

abundance left to thrive inside

The way fields sweep across the land

A cinema of small lives there

A ground hog lazy in the sun

Field mice with a place to run

And sometimes I like things that rhyme

and pace themselves to stop in time

as though they have some cool control—

(not found in my other world)

Poems, and patients, thriving fields

doctor my heart on being still

Ointment

There is the jar an ancestor left

slightly opened, a face paint made

from yellow dandelions and red roses

crushed into deep hints of color

Each morning I stain my face

into a healthy citizen, an almost

jovial glaze for a world view

I grow resilient and paint beneath

a thousand eyes that eventually

make their way to become my own

I stand strong and stare

at all the small flowers that dropped

into this final settling in a jar

Some days I am delicate

Some days I dig my fingers

in the crazy paint that is always

slightly opened

My spirit expanding and deflating

with gentleness and scars

Night

Night could not decipher

the solitude of my eyes

I was happy in the quiet

I loved the white stars trying

to imitate butterflies

Their pointed wings as bright

as moths in bright porch light

The sky grew blacker and brighter

and the wind slept alone

in the trees

Turning in the sighing way

Of all lonely things

Lullabies Of A Beggar Wind

The branches are knobbed, and green with bumps of
promises
And on some—the flowering is still holding tight to colors
that spill through tiny slits
I am listening to the lullabies stepping from tree to tree, and
to the birds lynching the breeze for strong flights
Everything lifts sideways, then upwards,
in a beggarly wind of tattered gusts
The sleeping hills awaken, and the circle
of life opens to a crucial newness
I am naming bright openings
in alphabetical order, and listening
to dreams and consequences
I pause on the letter of your name
Pretending for one moment that an opening
is still there—That somewhere you are listening
to the lullabies of the beggar wind and whistling
your way back home
But it is only a moment caught in the feathers
of the ragged wind catcher—slipping through in a flutter

Life Wings

She mentioned that by now I should have more clarity,

and know my visions inside out

But I go into myself and it is noisy, and I want out,

and I am out and it is so quiet that I go in

Is that clear? Is that what I am about?

Shoved this way and that—switching my sponsor hats

and trying to please so many producers

And nothing fits but the blue sky

riding a warm breeze through my hair

My back bends in a landlord's life of collecting

rents, and avoiding evictions

I owe the world something—or so it hints—

and I have ballads I place on a wooden seat

inside a knotted rope and swing

far out over a thousand walls

Songs fall, you know, and their legs kick wildly

in the fear of letting go

So I become a trumpet player for the love

of blowing gold in long blue denials

And I love everyone like moonlight

Splash a boogie like a rain dance

in star filled puddles and I hear the horn

and my feet and my arms passing notes

in all directions—until I free the stunned

trumpet from my sore, reddened lips

and I coddle my throat

to a joyful rendition of small life wings

I may know nothing or something about

No Glorious Plan

It's not that I have a glorious plan

I just like a metrical view, a vision

to keep things interesting

when the taxes are due, the food low,

some half claimed stray

needs an operation

that costs as much as my used car

I am acquainted with being poor

Still, there is something celestial

in the dusk that grows

into something solid in the dawn

A half remembered nostalgia

for something I lost somewhere,

a friendly conversation with a higher power

And I have constructed plans

that pressed their knees to the ground,

kept falling down, refused to be sold

on my cuddled references to gold

I have sent plans out halfcocked, too young,

beautiful in their naive appreciation,

turning against all obstacles, into good ones

Of course the gods laughed and scratched

my heart for a favor, nothing being free,

nothing able to press the clutch of destiny

One plan comes in, another goes out—

A suggestion, a jubilation, a small white lie—

a lunatic, a genius, all swerving to try.

I Need To Hear You Breathing

Too easy to drop in my cave of thoughts

and not come out for the morning light,

or for the traffic slowly jammed and following

one another in a stranger parade

Some nights are perfect in the oblivion of sleep,

and some days stay thrush and dove filled

with the humble small headed moments

wandering the ground in ruffled flutters

At this moment I need to hear you breathing

The wings of your lashes a golden red disarray

Your chest brown and rising again and again

in the steady promise of awakening

But it is quiet here with reality

and your large absence of calm empathy

And if I am not lost in the tangle of sheets

Neither am I found – Not now, not in this cache

Of maddening grief – Where I listen in silence

for the sound of your breath – and clinch my own

to a slow shallow of imperfect hope

Hermit In The Woods

Suddenly I am at pause

and you an arm's length

of apple bough kindness

The white fall of your hair

on stooped shoulders—

I follow you through fog

across the floor of rocks

where you hermit your life

in a turn against humanity

Leading the lostness

of my eyes to rightness

We part at the long pine

You return to a log chair

and paneless skies

and I turn south

Not finished yet with humanity

Budding again and again

with turns of company

and thinking often of you

snarled brown and white

beneath a blue moon

weary of the trenches

wealthy men shovel

Heart Wood Follies

Once, on an interior voyage, I saw the face of suicide crouched

inside my fingers, studying my wrists, and I made one small attempt

at reconciliation—But she asked too much, and I could not contend

with her downward trend—We were never meant to be friends.

Although an introvert lingered for years in my memory.

I am too intense, I overindulge in every emotion, I evaluate myself

from a distance, when I should be inside, running the show

I disparage too many needs, and play a keyboard late at night,

tapping a run of visions and songs that always go on too long

I never let go of anything if it begs to stay, though some things should be assessed, released, torn from the heart before damage

But I am damaged. My spirit criticizes my soul and my body is a landmine
with all the traps cleverly disguised, and when I weep, it could be
for anything, nothing ever falling below compassion, nothing ever cruel
enough to stop believing, that it might change, kneel, sob, ask for forgiveness
And my empathy is wasted most days—my eyes startled
by the sheer brand of toughness that makes it way, always,
into the middle of my heart, where I move aside furniture and places,
old toys and beloved faces, a forest and a mountain,
all for a lost poem on a slow boat to disappointment

Healing

I don't care about the length of time it takes to heal

I know the fallacy of that

The vertical memories and swift glimpses in darkened cor-

ners

The photos left smiling vacancies

To prove it, I monitor the amount of pepper sprinkling the

eggs

I watch a thorn rose bloom from beginning to end

I see the long blue of the lake splashing people on every

shore

Nothing bothers me, it is too hot, too cool, the ceiling drips

drywall that refuses to know its place

It is beneath me, it is a ragged edge around me, it the last

blackberries

with a brown tinge that the birds consider,

then rip from the vine with a vengeance

Angels In Trees

I can see flashes of elegant angels

in elaborate dresses at sunrise

They are standing in the trees

and pretending to be daybreak—

and unless you freelance your eyes

into the wide wingspan and blend of leaves

you can almost believe that to be so

But there are more translations here

than we know—and I am glad for brilliance,

and light that forms majestic silver

I am driving to escape the terrible

pain balloons that hover

over my head, cartoonish with distortion

and bursting with the implications of grief

I shake them away, and study tips of light

and search the trees for ambassadors of peace

I hold my hand out the window to the fresh

cold—An alert winter unfolds here

where my hair flies in electric high tuning

pulling upwards against the gravity of thoughts

that might lead to tightly hidden despair

I am glad for the healing light of angels—

Standing tall against the perfect sky

slipping hope through the openings

of my troubled morning eyes

Annie—In Your Forest

In your forest a silver crevasse of light

through the heavy trees

And you believe in its splendor

as an omen—a forbidden glimpse

of a good future—A shy vanishing

of the long thunder that roared

the narrow silhouettes of your life

And I believe it too

Annie—there is more energy

in the chambers of your heart

than you dream of now

The way you vanquish black branches

and search the open fields

for the beauty of wildflowers

I create what I will—but you—

have the gift of vanishing

beneath your silver winged hair

finding the small violet of beauty

your dreams left there.

Bella River

There is the river moist with morning

and the round eyes of birds searching

among the sprawled grasses

The last of the fog rolls away with its wide blue song

leaving a mist of memory all across the water

I am never chilled when the world is beautiful

Here it is possible to bind with believe and be kind

The sweet fern has no interest in animosity

and the carp do not dream of sorrow

Once I met a rainbow trout that flew

Long ways and upward into a bright beacon

I would be happy to have such an uprising

And share a quick kiss with the brilliant sun

Behind The Dumpster

Now who will find you

with your long hair tangled

in the street of false stars

Your face hollowed beneath the cloak

of long nights that swallow

piece by piece of your free will

Who will mend your fragile bones

shivering in the winter of highs

when you tremble with deception

One small light glowing in your heart

A golden memory flickering

in the dull corner of brick and dark

Who will wash your face with a soft cloth

while you point out the culprit

with a delicate hand

Your eyes large and black in the silence

One small light flickering its way out

Crow Heart

Too blue black to show your bruising

you lift into the sky billows of morning rose

A soft plume of underbelly feathers

buried beneath tough wings

You dip for the residue of silos

and Carolina corn hardened to seed

All that is beautiful in your sheen dies

in the thievery of your reputation

and I cannot help but note

the pacing from limb to limb

And sudden swoops of bravado

in a determination of hard eyes

Are you weary yet, blackbird

Tormented by the rags of false men

that keep you circling far too long

always too alert for peaceful planning

and one black flight away from resting

February Evening

Wandering through a February evening

My mind a ferry of back and forth

I am thinking of the raspberry bushes

behind the yellow house where we lived

Lushly hidden in foliage and trees,

but so alive in spring

They are bulldozed now into a flat clay dullness

for the opening of a plaza

Our city fell in love with that kind of magic

I am watching the mountains stretch

an implication of strength

across the gray and rose loveliness

of a dragon horizon

I am too pensive at dusk

Seeing the road in the valley curve

with the headlights of movement

and the smooth flow of so many

plans going somewhere

I am too back and forth between

raspberries and mountains

My eyes captured in the petit mal

of an inner stare

Staying still as the wind moves

too many things that were once sure

Finch

It is too cold here and I am

half tired in the white morning

where the pines stand like apostles

their long arms touching ground

A decorum of quiet gray cannot find light

and the gospel of bird song stays quiet

some birds paralyzed with frost

but not the yellow finch, it flies the sun

from tree to tree

Yellow, in this light, is alien to see

Flying The Night Ropes

I fly from the top of the tent

and the platform shakes with warnings

But I have cast out, and the first swing

is always the hardest

I have the momentum, I have the grace

I scorn the net that believes I will fall

There is a catcher who knows my heart,

my hands, and swings toward my grasp

I am a flyer with arthritic fingers —

but only two! Two chances to fail —

There is never really a third

The catcher grabs my wrists, and

then let's go,

so I fly straight up, and turn, turn, to fly wide

in a perfect arc, above the love

of the crowd,

the gasp at my easy perfection, the warmth of lights

far brighter than the incandescent sun,

and I turn

back to my pedestal, where I land, and stand,

hand tight on the rope,

the other in a friendly free wave

As the pain in my fingers throbs

in a twosome of swollen rage

but I have always paid,

for all my strength in flying

All the freedom lies in trying.

Words On Water

I can ask the river anything

but how can it hear with

water in its ears—the current

constant in an onward roll?

It is on a round trip journey

Eventually my words return to me—

Cleanly changed by water and time

Their reverence now purged

by the miles—things only important

until the next thing

Life with no hesitancy whatsoever

hitting rocks, and sliding

in and out of deep water

Walking Wings

I am sewing the silk stitches of air

into a morning walk

The clouds are out—moving in slow billows

Some are gray with the indecisiveness of rain

The newspaper, thrown in orange plastic

confirms the threat

If I had wings I could move leisurely,

for there are hills here to travel,

but the morning breath of tall trees

can be uplifting,

and my feet do well enough in wandering

Today I move slowly—I am a water bird

with water beads rolling down my lengthy neck

There is the flutter of an asylum of ducks

wild with the beauty and power of large feet

They are dipping their heads in water

lifting them out and upwards in long swallows

Frogs practice the same song

someone always off key—so that

they must start over

The birds sing sharply to one another

in a rapid shrapnel of voices

and I am simply walking—and watching.

Sea Legs

The shrimp boats with their white flag

of seagulls flows across the water

I can see them and almost hear the feet

of the men rushing, and the voices

cursing or praising a catch

No churning, shouting, cutting

in the salt wind—only a cold breeze

on a clear afternoon of blue aching

in the bones of the heart

I offer that last part to the scenic day

and wish for the better judgment

of an optimist with a thick book

holding good cheer in earmarked pages

Instead I am sullen with myself, grayish

with the feel of salt in my shoes

and throwing shells as quickly

as they wash ashore

Back into the rolling laughter

of an indifferent sea

The waves rushing like bullies

toward the new kid on the beach

as defenseless as a shell

too light weight to swim free

Sea Girl

She was stubbornly a seal

and would not leave the ice

when the men approached

Sticks killed her mother—

sticks broke her blood

but she crawled exultant

toward the water

Wanting nothing to do here

with the hard and cruel

Wanting only the cool

of moderate water

The world a bigger corruption

than she had bargained for

Split

The trees grow dark and rap a knuckle on the window

Behind their green eyes the mountains go on forever

I am looking inside now—An English woman, an Irish woman,

a small Cherokee, all nod and watch my medusa hands

I am made for the hearth, a cornerstone, a solid piece

I am loved for work, the crook of my elbow, the soft eye

on a frail neck and fearful spine

And yet there is a meadow where music plays, and the juiciest

peach falls from the tree—There is a May day dance

and a cardinal dallying with a young fox, newly a mother,

but romping the grass on her playfully important journey

When no one is watching, I am on a journey too

I wear turquoise and white and lure all the spring water

over stones

I am strong in the beautiful way of the randomly destroyed

and whitewash dungeons to a gloss

I have built a city of friends with interesting faces,

and we listen to the piano in an open field

If you call me, I answer, my mind arrested

by the stricken eyes of the world—and I will help

earnestly, it is my common role—

to mend the broken strings as they tighten

into the yarn ball that keeps this world small

I Have An Ark

I have an ark with a spectacular view

The spine of it is lined with books

I have sealed the boards with honey

There is a soft rug by a leather chair

I sleep on the floor for better stretching

I have a small river that runs into a larger sea

Gray doves have built a nest in the far eave.

This is my special scroll I found

buried beneath the roots of a pale birch

Nothing is written on it but possibilities.

Have you heard the wind song of dawn?

Each morning she plays a blue pipe.

All the birds sing slightly off key.

It is the way their individual songs drop

from the varying height of branches.

There is a puppet of myself in the southern sky.

Some days I pull the strings of repetition.

It is little more than a ritual.

Angels stare from the laurel bushes.

Their eyes flower large and white.

Sometimes the church will bring someone

to hold under the river

They lift them from the water

singing praise, praise, holy.

Swamp Flower

There in the oily green of swamp

drifts a lovely lily rose,

unthorned on thickened pads of float

The slippery frog a constant friend

They call the water there unclean

Still, it is true that lovely things

can grow in molds of ugliness

Hidden in the hard wood forest

and glistening in the sun's warm touch

Hidden

The tassels of the sun push through

and the pleated leaves forget

they were rained upon

A large belt of the river is visible

and shining in small places

Somewhere at the water's bottom

a carp lies still as mud

He is so immeasurably warm there

that he believes

sun strikes on the water to be a storm

Don't Be Afraid

I am trying to tell you courageous things

an attempted sorcery from better years

a softer blend into

your silent litany of fears

You must not panic or checker your heart

with bits of odd confusion, unwelcome thoughts

If you want a story—Yes, it is just us.

We are sailing and the wind rides

through the blue cheeked clouds

It cools the sweaty spot beneath

the red shine of your auburn hair

You are brown and brave in a white shirt

and it flutters faster than the gull's flight

See how free we channel into the ocean

of great fortune and everything prettier

than it has ever been

Everything sky wide with fun and warm sun!

Here! Look here! No melancholy now!

You know the treachery

of a stray thought, a worried frown

Don't worry that the water is too wild

Embrace the flying confetti

of the wind-flung foam

the sea's offering of kisses

in a wave of white plumes

Bluebirds

I envy their sky

held close and softly feathered

I can see they mean to keep

blue within their reach

Black clouds pass them by

I envy their sky

The Last Seahorse

This woman that I knew, she walked,

each morning by the ocean's edge

She watched the coral wash come in

and set her hopes up in the sand.

Her footprints scarcely glazed the wet,

but followed closely, vague as wax

Sometimes she would amuse herself

with six piece settings made of shell,

thin wishes set for someone else.

She was not lovely in the way

society wished women to be,

her beauty rose from somewhere else,

close quartered in an inward depth,

she took long views on godliness.

She was too ragged for requests,

so tourists seldom edged her strand

of silent, contemplative sand

But still, she knew the sun and tides

and all the heights the ocean rode

She knew the salt that dried her skin

in constant blows of offshore winds

She knew the brightest days could end

with rain torrents brought by the sea,

as old seahorses fell to bleach,

in sand pockets on Hindsight Beach

Women in the Snow

Yesterday on the beach

she was a sea gull

a seal heart

a short coat unbuttoned

and reading aloud

In the spring she read

a bridal magazine

chose house shoes

flung long soulful looks

into the large square

of the picture window

where golden rings tightened

around the drapery drawback

around her finger

around the crime scene

where the victim lay

But she had witnessed

women in the snow

in the tarot card

in an ice storm

in the restaurants of bad backs

and the faces of laurels

withering in the cold

The women in the snow

held empty bowls

and sturdy shoes they carried

in large bags

beside the sweet talk of a loser

They cultivated gray matter

and spoke like wood chopping

on a dull stump

Some of the women screamed

in the snow with children

They were in agony

they got their feet wet

they threw shrill vowels

when the children vomited

They stuck lost kisses

on apartment shelves

But the way she wanted out

was in a strong wind, on a reindeer,

in the backseat of Santa's sled

with a moisturizer and a manicure

and a mirror that held a light inside

She wanted five hundred feet

from ocean front

in a short coat,

unbuttoned,

with a seal heart and a sea gull

and a new start

in a palm tree with a sun beam

with a red flower

and a book sleeve

where she could read

or she could write

'til her eyes fell

on a fairytale

that she struck down

with a sea weed

then she read the part

in the gray print

where the brain lived

and she stayed there

'til she grew up again

where the only rings

were around the sun

and around her head

when the hot breeze

and her hair flew

in the beggar wind.

Notice To A Friend

There is a static in the mind, and suddenly

it breaks into a full blown dandelion

The status changes as the pieces fly

into indistinct constellations

And the guilt flies in one direction,

and the shame in another

as the raw headlights of sunlight

watch furtively from behind the stars

All feeling sings the song of cicadas

high pitched in a radar toward white light

I once watched this from a pier

too near the ocean to hear anything

but the steady roar of water slapping

arched backs against the boards

Something broke and the scattering

flew in a selection of directions

And it seemed all directions called

The mind broke and the white noise

was gusting toward a large hail

that simmered eventually into an easy breeze

There is nothing else I can say

This may happen more than once

before the sunlight brings back

your hardy red days

Was She Pretty?

During my internship at the mental hospital,

a young woman greeted me, day after day,

to ask if she was pretty and if I loved her.

I said, yes. yes.

because she was pretty and because

I wanted to please her, and affection

is not that difficult to distribute, especially

if you have been given plenty of it.

So each day she abducted my attention

and wondered if I might be her sister

and did I have a boyfriend or a baby?

and would I be her friend, would I be her friend,

Would I Be Her Friend?

I said yes, yes, yes.

and she said, here…

and handed me a comb

so I combed her hair.

I touched her hair and she grew still.

sometimes she would reach up

and touch my fingers on the comb

and follow the strokes down

sometimes she would hold her head

all the way back so that she could stare

into my face

and always, do you love me, in that voice

of child— —like desperation,

as she searched for someone I might be,

or may have been, long ago.

her hair was beautiful and brown.

Before I left there, she pulled the plaster

from a high, barred window

and used it as a knife

so the aides hurried and took her to isolation,

the last place she had meant to be,

as though isolation would cure

that terrible need.

I wish someone had combed her hair

all of her life. Her hair was shiny

and very, very, brown.

Night Shades

A vivacious night fan blowing

One star has deliberately hidden

behind another

as the drapes marry in a tango

and a sway toward morning

I spread like smoke to waver

at the edge of dreams

There is a humidity that has cooled

into a heavy silence

The birds tuck their heads

and songs beneath feathers

Somewhere the night train idles

into a long, last whistle

About the Author

Phibby Venable's work has been published in 2River, Poetrybay, Southern Ocean Review, Sow's Ear, Voices, the Appalachian Journal and various other national & international magazines.

The proceeds of her book, Indian Wind Song, were used to help low income Appalachian families with indoor plumbing and home repairs. Venable won the Virginia Water Project Award, and was nominated for the governor's award for Volunteer Excellence. She is active in animal rescue.

She was nominated by Goldfish Press for the Pushcart Prize in 2009, and in 2010 by Quill and Parchment Press. She is the author of Women of the Round Table, a novel, and Dry Branch Hollow, a collection of short stories.

ALL THINGS THAT MATTER PRESS

FOR MORE INFORMATION ON TITLES AVAILABLE FROM

ALL THINGS THAT MATTER PRESS, GO TO

http://allthingsthatmatterpress.com

or contact us at

allthingsthatmatterpress@gmail.com

If you enjoyed this book, please post a review on Amazon.com

and your favorite social media sites.

Thank you!

www.ingramcontent.com/pod-product-compliance
Lightning Source LLC
Chambersburg PA
CBHW060456090426
42735CB00011B/2008

9780996663441